Healing
the
Wounded
GIANT

Healing
the
Wounded
GIANT

Maintaining Military Preeminence
While Cutting the Defense Budget

Michael E. O'Hanlon

BROOKINGS INSTITUTION PRESS
Washington, D.C.

Library of Congress Cataloging-in-Publication data is available.
ISBN: 978-0-8157-2485-8

9 8 7 6 5 4 3 2 1

Printed on acid-free paper

Typeset in Sabon

Composition by R. Lynn Rivenbark
Macon, Georgia

Printed by R. R. Donnelley
Harrisonburg, Virginia

For Bob Faherty,
with immeasurable gratitude,

and in memory of
Hal Sonnenfeldt

CONTENTS

PREFACE

How much more should defense spending be cut, if at all, as part of further deficit reduction efforts in the United States? This is a central question as Congress and the president seek to avoid future fiscal calamities while finding a balanced, politically acceptable path toward deficit reduction.

The cuts initially mandated from the 2011 Budget Control Act are often described as costing the armed forces $487 billion over ten years, relative to the plan that existed before that deal was passed. In fact, it is more accurate to describe those cuts as totaling $350 billion, since that is the total when the current defense plan is measured relative to a standard Congressional Budget Office baseline that assumes only adjustments for inflation into the future. Savings from reduced war spending are even larger, and additional to the $350 billion figure—though, of course, that spending was never intended to be permanent and as such should be analyzed separately.

Should it remain in place, the March 2013 sequestration, like the recommendations of the Simpson-Bowles and Rivlin-Domenici deficit reduction commissions of 2010, would cut roughly another $500 billion from defense spending levels over the next ten years.

The Obama administration's military plan, as published in early 2012, now incorporates the assumed cuts from the first round of the Budget Control Act—the $350 billion noted above. It does not include cuts from sequestration. The current administration plan will scale down the military from about 1.5 million active-duty uniformed personnel to its pre-9/11 total of 1.4 million, or two-thirds the cold war norm. It chips away at modernization programs but preserves most major ones, with one or two notable exceptions. It levels off various forms of military pay and benefits. But most troops will continue to be compensated better than private-sector cohorts of similar age, education, and technical skill. The Obama plan also holds out ambitious hopes for efficiencies from various vaguely specified reforms projected to save $60 billion over a decade, and it assumes, again optimistically, that weapons systems will be delivered at currently projected costs. Overall, the 2012 Obama plan amounts to a serious belt tightening, rather than fundamental strategic or military change.

Conceptually, the Obama approach is built on time-tested principles of American defense policy, modified only modestly in recent years. The Persian Gulf and Western Pacific remain the two principal theaters of overseas concern—although the administration is seeking to emphasize the broader Middle East/Gulf region somewhat less than in the past and, through its policy of "rebalancing," the Pacific somewhat more. A two-war capability of sorts is retained, even if two full-scale simultaneous regional conflicts are assessed as less likely than before, and large-scale stabilization missions are also seen as less likely. Of course, these latter assumptions must be tempered by the fact that possible enemies get a say in our decisions, too. In the short term, force planning must also account for two specific matters of acute concern: the ongoing operation in Afghanistan, where more than 60,000 American troops remain as of early 2013, and possible operations in the coming year or two against Iran's nuclear facilities. Surprises could lurk, too.

Against this backdrop, this book argues that it is possible to imagine additional defense cuts, in weapons and force structure and other expenses, of up to $200 billion over a decade, above and beyond those scheduled in 2012. These savings, however, would be considerably less than envisioned under sequestration or Simpson-Bowles.

Moreover, some of those savings might be counterbalanced by higher-than-expected costs in the Department of Defense (DoD). What this means is that net savings could be less than $200 billion, perhaps by tens of billions of dollars—an important reality to bear in mind in all discussions of future defense reforms. We may need to cut more forces and weapons just to achieve the budget targets already assumed by existing law and policy as of 2012.

My recommendations include the following:

—The size of the active-duty Army and Marine Corps could be reduced modestly below their 1990s levels (to, say, 450,000 soldiers and 160,000 Marines); plans as of 2012 are to keep them slightly above those levels. Ten-year savings relative to the administration's 2012 plans could reach about $80 billion.

—Rather than increase its fleet, the Navy could employ innovative approaches like "sea swap," by which some crews are rotated via airplane while ships stay forward-deployed longer. This idea, and more forward homeporting of attack submarines at Guam, could eventually allow the Navy to get by with 260 to 270 ships rather than 286. Ten-year savings could be $25 billion.

—The F-35 joint strike fighter, a good plane but an expensive one, could be scaled back by half from its current intended buy of about 2,500 airframes, at an eventual annual savings of more than $5 billion but with only modest cumulative savings of $10 billion to $20 billion over the coming decade (as some planes should be bought promptly).

—Rather than designing a new submarine to carry ballistic missiles, the Navy might simply refurbish the existing Trident submarine or reopen that production line. That and other economies in nuclear forces, including the conversion of Lawrence Livermore National Laboratories away from the nuclear weapons design business, could yield $20 billion in ten-year savings in the national defense budget. Cancellation of a short-range missile defense program could save another $7 billion or so.

—Military compensation could be streamlined further as well, despite Congress's recent reluctance to go along with even the modest changes proposed in 2012 by the administration. Stateside commissaries and exchanges might be closed, and military health care premiums increased even more than the administration proposed last year. Military pensions might be reformed too, with somewhat lower payments for working-age military retirees having twenty years or more of service, and introduction of a 401k-like plan for those who never reach twenty years (and currently receive nothing). This could be done in a way that would achieve modest net savings. The combined effects of all these changes could exceed $50 billion over ten years.

Another idea in this vein could save substantial sums, although it would require help from allies and would have to be phased in with time. At present the United States relies almost exclusively on aircraft carriers, each carrying about seventy-two aircraft, to have short-range jets in position for possible conflict with Iran. Over the past decade, land-based combat jets formerly based in Saudi Arabia, Kuwait, and Iraq have largely come home. While the United States occasionally rotates fighter jets through the small states of the Gulf Cooperation Council, and while it maintains command and control and support assets in states like Qatar and the United Arab Emirates, permanent ashore combat power is very limited. By seeking two or more places to station Air Force combat jets continuously in Gulf states, the United States could facilitate a reduction of one or two carrier battle groups in its fleet. (In theory, it could cut the aircraft carrier fleet even more this way, since the Navy currently needs about five carriers in the fleet to sustain one always on station. But the unpredictabilities of such foreign basing counsel a more hedged approach—for example, if Gulf states refused permission, the United States might need to surge carriers temporarily even under this plan to conduct offensive operations against Iranian nuclear facilities.) Cutting two aircraft carrier battle groups and associated aircraft could save perhaps $50 billion over a decade, since this option would take time to implement even if regional allies quickly approve it.

Other more modest changes—for example scaling back purchases of the Littoral Combat Ship, curtailing production of the V-22 Osprey, carrying out another round of base closures, streamlining the acquisition workforce by reducing paperwork requirements, adopting best practices for weapons maintenance more widely, and modestly constraining intelligence spending—could save perhaps a total of $40 billion to $50 billion over a decade.

Taking everything together, gross ten-year savings from all of the ideas mentioned above could approach $250 billion, if it actually proved possible to implement them in the face of likely congressional and allied skepticism about some of them. In fact, it would be quite ambitious to achieve up to $200 billion in reductions in military units and weapons programs and other costs, relative to what is now planned as of early 2013. And again, it should be underscored that the net savings in overall defense spending levels might not be quite that high. At present, DoD plans are probably optimistic in the savings they foresee from currently anticipated changes. That means some additional programmatic cuts could be needed just to comply with defense budget caps that are already in place under the initial provisions of the 2011 Budget Control Act.

Further defense cuts should be viewed in a tempered, moderate way. They are not inconceivable, even if the United States retains its current grand strategy and basic military policy. But they should not approach the deep levels foreseen by either sequestration or plans like that of the Simpson-Bowles commission. While hardly emasculating the country or its armed forces, such cuts would be too risky, given the world in which we live.

ACKNOWLEDGMENTS

The author wishes to thank Ted Piccone, Peter Singer, John Barnett, and Ian Livingston for their assistance in the writing and editing of this book. Thanks too for additional inspiration and guidance from Martin Indyk, Ken Lieberthal, Ken Pollack, and Robert Kagan.

Colleagues in other parts of Brookings have been hugely helpful too, starting with Alice Rivlin and Ron Haskins, and including also Bruce Katz, Amy Liu, Barry Bosworth, Bill Gale, Belle Sawhill, Gary Burtless, Henry Aaron, William Galston, Rebecca Winthrop, Carol Graham, Brendan Orino, Steven Pifer, and Bruce Riedel. Outside of Brookings, Maya MacGuineas and Bob Reischauer have as always taught me a great deal about the budget and defense, as have Richard Betts, Stephen Biddle, Michael Berger, Wayne Glass, Lane Pierrot, Fran Lussier, David Mosher, Rachel Schmidt, Ellen Breslin-Davidson, Jack Mayer, and Bob Hale.

I would like to thank the Sasakawa Peace Foundation, as well as Herb Allen, Marshall Rose, Casey Wasserman, Mala Gaonkar, members of the Brookings national security industrial base working group, and several anonymous donors for important support.

1

AMERICAN MILITARY STRATEGY AND GRAND STRATEGY

American national security strategy is premised on international presence, deterrence, and engagement. Jarred by the world wars into recognizing that its geographic isolation from most of the world's industrial and resource centers did not allow it to stay out of other nations' conflicts, the United States chose to stay active internationally after World War II. It developed a network of alliances throughout Western Europe, East Asia, parts of the broader Middle East, and Latin America.

At times the United States was arguably not quick enough to form alliances, as when deterrence failed and North Korea invaded South Korea in 1950. At other times it forged partnerships with regimes that did not share its values or lacked staying power, as with the Shah's Iran or the government of South Vietnam. But for the most part, U.S. security partnerships endured. Even after the cold war ended, the United States retained this system of alliances. The rise of new dangers, such as the proliferation of nuclear weapons, as well as ongoing threats posed by hostile regimes in North Korea,

Iran, and Iraq, made American disengagement seem an imprudent option—for the United States and for its security partners as well. Indeed, in playing its worldwide military role, the United States has more than sixty formal allies or other close security partners with whom it teams in one way or another.

This set of partnerships and overseas commitments sounds enormously ambitious and costly. In some ways, it surely is. Defending only America's own territory would be feasible at far less cost, with far fewer forces, than maintenance of this global network—at least for a while. But the costs of war can be far greater, in lives and treasure, than the costs of preparedness and deterrence. As such, the United States has now sustained a standing military at an average annual cost of some $475 billion (expressed in constant or inflation-adjusted 2013 dollars) for more than half a century. At present it spends some $650 billion, though those numbers are gradually declining under current law and policy, as the war in Afghanistan winds down. By mid-decade, national defense budget and spending levels will trend toward $550 billion a year (excluding Veterans Administration expenses, but including most intelligence functions and Department of Energy nuclear weapons activities). Sequestration, as required by the 2011 Budget Control Act unless superseded, or similar plans would reduce that latter annual figure to about $500 billion (again, as expressed in constant 2013 dollars).

This book searches for responsible ways to cut defense a bit more. It concludes that sequestration, or plans like the 2010 Simpson-Bowles deficit reduction proposal, would cut the military too deeply. That said, there is room for further economizing that would allow moderately significant additional cuts in weapons, forces, and compensation levels, as well as administrative reforms and efficiencies—totaling up to $200 billion over a decade in gross terms. Net savings in the overall national security budget might be $100 billion to $150 billion—a modest, but hardly insignificant, contribution toward the $2.5 trillion or so in ten-year federal deficit reduction that many economists consider advisable prior to sequestration. Taken together, these planned and suggested changes would result in an annual national defense spending level of perhaps $525 billion to $535 billion.

The Economic Challenge to American Security

The recent run of trillion-dollar federal deficits, coupled with the deep recession of 2008–09 and a still-sluggish economy, has contributed to the anxieties Americans have about the future; many lost their homes and jobs, have seen their investment portfolios shrink, and have lost faith in the American dream. For foreign policy strategists, these worries are compounded by a sense that throughout history, great powers with weakening economic foundations cannot stay great powers for long. In a democracy like America's, the economic problem is compounded by the political risk that as fewer citizens perceive personal benefit from America's strategy of internationalism, their support for continued engagement abroad can be expected to weaken. Such tendencies are already seen in a number of demographic and socioeconomic groups, including in the attitudes of younger generations today.[1] And as great powers decline or fall, others generally seek to fill the resulting power vacuum—resulting not only in diminished influence for the former power, but greater instability and risk for the international system on the whole, since war is often the result.

As such, while defense cuts must be made, they must be made carefully. It would be unwise to spend more on defense than is necessary, but it would be penny-wise and pound-foolish to jeopardize the general stability of today's international system in an overly assertive effort to reduce the U.S. federal deficit by some specific percentage. Perhaps interstate war has become unthinkable today. But that theory was voiced in earlier eras, only to be proven wrong by subsequent events, as when Norman Angell's prediction that economic interlinkages made war unthinkable was invalidated shortly thereafter by the outbreak of World War I.[2] Maybe the twentieth century's experiences—huge casualties from the world wars and huge projected casualties in any future war involving nuclear weapons—have taught mankind the risks of armed conflict. But it is hardly inconceivable that new sources of conflict could emerge—over disputed seabed resources, over the uneven effects of climate change on different countries and regions, over nuclear or biological weapons dangers or threats.[3]

China's rise is causing tectonic shifts in the international power distribution as well. One need not be a Sinophobe to understand that changes of the current magnitude can be destabilizing; at least, that has been the historical tendency in other periods of hegemonic transformation. China is on balance acting reasonably responsibly in most domains of international affairs. But its very rise produces temptations at home and insecurities abroad. Its recent behavior in the South China Sea as well as the East China Sea suggests certain ambitions, particularly among its often nationalistic and anti-American military leadership. One need not expect to fight China to believe that it is important to retain strong American capabilities and American alliances to preserve a stable existing order as China continues to reach toward likely superpower status.[4]

Robust U.S. defense spending levels are surely preferable to a major-power war or other serious conflict. Nor do they seem inherently dangerous. The United States already has enough checks on its uses of force, including general aversion to casualties, as well as a desire to look inward and focus on domestic issues rather than expend resources abroad, that it is probably not necessary to cut defense in order somehow to prevent unwanted military operations. The United States of modern times is not exactly a peaceful nation, and it is certainly not pacifist. But neither is it an imperialistic country, as traditionally defined.

Yes, the United States invaded Iraq without desirable levels of international support or legitimacy. And that war may be seen as unwise by history. But if that was the worst thing that modern America could do—invading a country to overthrow one of the world's worst dictators who was in violation of the terms of the 1991 ceasefire ending Operation Desert Storm and more than a dozen UN Security Council resolu-

Figure 1-1. *China's Gross Domestic Product (PPP), 1980–2011*

Billions of 2013 dollars

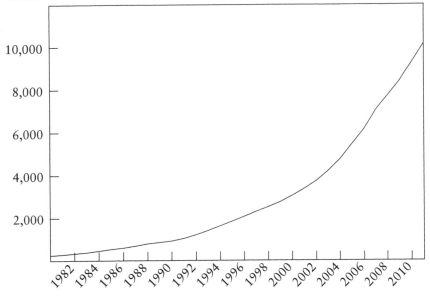

Note: Purchasing Power Parity (PPP) figures are somewhat greater than GDP measured by official nominal exchange rates. For comparison, U.S. GDP (PPP) in 2010 was $14,582 billion. The Carnegie Endowment projects China's real GDP to reach $23,358 billion in 2025 and $46,348 billion in 2050.

Sources: The World Bank Group, World DataBank (2013) (http://databank.worldbank. org); Zbigniew Brzezinski, *Strategic Vision: America and the Crisis of Global Power* (New York: Basic Books, 2012), p. 57.

tions—it is easy to see why more than sixty countries still ally with the United States even as they sometimes harshly disagree with it. American power is apparently perceived by others as desirable and stabilizing, as also reflected in the fact that no hostile or opposing bloc of nations has formed against it.[5]

If having a smaller military guaranteed that the country would avoid mistakes about the use of force, while having enough capability to prevail in smart wars, most people would presumably assent to that arrangement. However, history does not tend to back up such a theory. Moreover, during some of the times when the United Stats was at its maximum national power, as during the Reagan years, it went to war

Figure 1-2. *China's Gross Domestic Product (PPP) as Share of World Gross Domestic Product, 1980–2011*

Percent

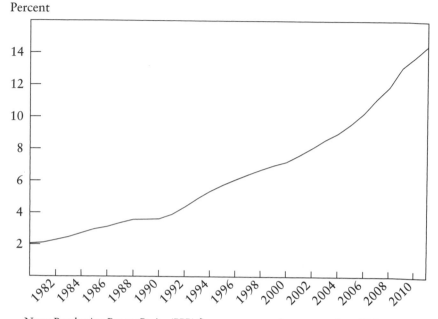

Note: Purchasing Power Parity (PPP) figures are somewhat greater than GDP measured by official nominal exchange rates. According to the Organization for Economic Cooperation and Development, the United States made up 23 percent of the world's GDP (PPP) in 2011. In 2030 the OECD projects China to make up 28 percent of the world's GDP (PPP), compared to 18 percent in the United States. In 2060 the projections keep China at 28 percent of the world's GDP (PPP) while dropping the United States to 16 percent.

Sources: The World Bank Group, World DataBank (2013) (http://databank.worldbank. org); Organization for Economic Cooperation and Development, "Economic Outlook No 91 — Long-Term Baseline Projection," June 2012.

relatively infrequently, or engaged only in low-level conflicts. So it hardly appears that having a strong military makes America more prone to adventurism, or that having a smaller and less costly military necessarily improves the odds of peace

Some people favor asking U.S. allies to do more, thereby enabling the United States to do less. That sentiment might seem to be sensible. But allies are sovereign and make their own decisions. As such, the alternative to current policy is not simply asking allies to do more, which Washington already does frequently, but to leave them to fend

Figure 1-3. *China's Military Expenditures, 1996–2011*

Billions of 2013 dollars

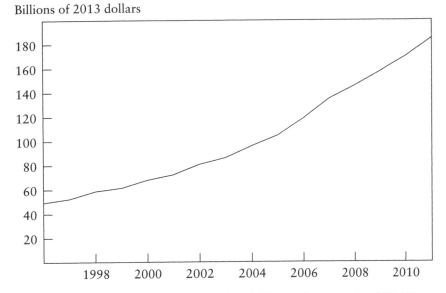

Note: The Pentagon's range for 2011 was $120 billion to a little more than $180 billion. Given previous estimates, I have used the higher number. Estimates by the International Institute for Strategic Studies (IISS), as reported in its annual The Military Balance, are about one-third lower per year than those reported by the Department of Defense. In 2011 the IISS's estimate for China's military expenditure was $111 billion. By 2030, based on GDP projections, China's military budget could reach $500 billion if it remains steady as a fraction of GDP.

Sources: Office of the Secretary of Defense, "Military and Security Developments Involving the People's Republic of China 2010" (Washington, August 2010), p. 42; "Military and Security Developments Involving the People's Republic of China 2011" (Washington, August 2011), p. 41 (www.defense.gov/pubs/pdfs/2011_CMPR_Final.pdf); "Military and Security Developments Involving the People's Republic of China 2011" (Washington, August 2012), p. 6 (www.defense.gov/pubs/pdfs/).

more for themselves and hope that they pick up the slack of American retrenchment. That would be a major strategic gamble. In places like the Persian Gulf, such an approach could easily produce conventional and nuclear arms races if countries such as Saudi Arabia and Turkey sought to counter Iran (and each other). Similar dynamics also could ensue among Japan, Korea, and China in East Asia. History suggests that such arms races do not tend to end well. For all the turbulence in today's world, American power would still seem stabilizing, as there have been no large-scale great-power wars since 1945. Put differently,

Iran does not have the capacity and China does not have the inclination to challenge American power directly at present. However, those states might well seek to challenge and dominate their regional neighbors absent compelling American security guarantees. War that ultimately dragged in the United States could well be the result.

Matters more mundane than global power balances also affect defense budget decisions. In considering possible reductions to the military budget, it is important to remember that most defense costs—for personnel, health care, environmental restoration, equipment maintenance, equipment modernization, and the like—go up faster than general inflation. In fact, the Congressional Budget Office (CBO) estimates that the average annual defense budget requirement for the next two decades will be about 10 percent greater than planned levels, with costs for operations, maintenance, and personnel collectively growing 1.5 percent a year faster than inflation over the period.[6] It is for that reason that I warn that some of the additional cuts in weapons, forces, and other Department of Defense expenses proposed below may be needed simply to comply with the initial budget caps of the 2011 Budget Control Act that were already in the books as of February 2013 (before sequestration). Just to "tread water," in other words, the Pentagon needs real budget growth of 1 to 2 percent, above the rate of inflation.

Some might quarrel with this, wondering why very large reductions are not possible for a military that has nearly doubled its real spending since 9/11, from around $400 billion in 2001 to around $700 billion annually a decade later and now some $650 billion (expressed in 2013 dollars). The answer is that, of that $300 billion in real growth in the annual budget, more than half was for wars that are ending (with resulting budget cuts already well under way). Of the remaining $125 billion or so, some was eaten up by higher per capita costs in areas such as health care. And about half of that amount, or some $60 billion to $70 billion in annual spending, was needed to reverse the "procurement holiday" that the country had enjoyed in the 1990s. The Reagan buildup had left us with large stocks of new equipment. By the George

Figure 1-4. *Federal Debt Held by the Public, 1940–2023*

Billions of 2013 dollars

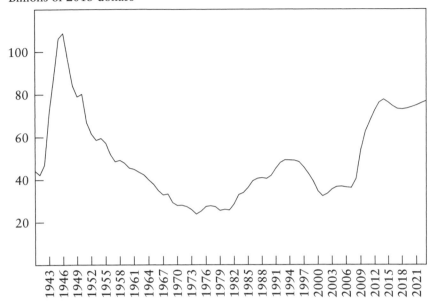

Note: Projections begin in 2013. These projections assume the current laws that govern federal taxes and spending do not change (as of February 2013), including sequestration.

Sources: Congressional Budget Office, *The Budget and Economic Outlook: Fiscal Years 2013 to 2023*, February 5, 2013 (www.cbo.gov/publication/43907).

W. Bush years, that equipment was aging and in need of replacement, so procurement budgets had to go back up. Unfortunately, we have not yet bought enough new equipment to have the luxury of going back to Clinton-era budget levels.[7] There is waste, and room for reform, but the amounts of savings ripe for easy harvest are not as great as some allege.

Such are the arguments in favor of avoiding big new cuts in U.S. defense spending. But of course, that is not the only side of the story. At the same time, it is also true that major American deficit reduction is necessary for the country's long-term strength. Former chairman of the Joint Chiefs of Staff Admiral Mike Mullen, former secretary of defense Robert Gates, and former secretary of state Hillary Rodham Clinton have all identified U.S. deficit and debt levels as major national security threats, and they are all surely right.[8] Mullen has even called the debt the nation's "biggest security threat."[9] While that claim can be debated, the broader point remains.

Some argue that military spending should be selectively protected, and currently planned cuts even reversed, as part of national deficit reduction efforts. But even from a national security perspective, that argument is problematic. The deficit reduction debate is a difficult one that can only engender political consensus when there exists a sense of shared sacrifice and comprehensive national belt-tightening. That is the lesson of the major deficit reduction efforts of the late 1980s and early 1990s, when taxes and military budgets and domestic spending were all part of the deficit-reduction effort. If some defense hawks were to succeed in excluding the Pentagon budget from the nation's fiscal reform efforts, the most likely outcomes would be a less successful deficit reduction outcome, growing debt, inadequate investment in the nation's economic fundamentals, and over time a weaker country with less national security. This is not to say that defense spending should take it on the chin. The 2011 Budget Control Act mistakenly placed most of the short-term burden of deficit reduction on the back of the Pentagon (as well as domestic discretionary accounts also important for long-term national power, since they fund science, infrastructure, education, and the like). But defense spending cannot be excluded from the deficit reduction effort either.

At a political level, too, the American public is likely ready for a period of less assertive foreign policy. The relative desirability of "wars of choice" probably will be seen—and should be seen—as lower in the future than it may have been in the past.[10] The trick is to reflect this sentiment without going too far.

Some toss around numbers to make their case that the United States either overspends or underspends on defense. These arguments are common, usually among those with a predetermined agenda of either making the defense budget seem high or low.

Those who wish to defend the magnitude of Pentagon spending often point out that in recent decades the military's share of the nation's economy has been modest by historical standards. During the 1960s, national defense spending was typically 8 to 9 percent of gross domestic product or GDP, declining to just under 5 percent by the late 1970s. During the Reagan buildup of the 1980s it reached 6 percent of GDP before declining to around 3 percent by the late 1990s after the cold war ended. During the first term of George W. Bush, the figure rose and ultimately approached 5 percent of GDP, but is now again headed back down and will soon be just over 3 percent. Seen in this light, current levels, even including wartime supplemental budgets, seem relatively moderate.[11]

On the other hand, those who criticize the Pentagon budget often note that it constitutes almost half of aggregate global military spending, and that American allies contribute another one-third or more of the total.[12] Or they note that recent defense spending levels, attaining at one point $700 billion a year, exceeded the cold war inflation-adjusted spending average of $475 billion by about 50 percent (when all figures are expressed in inflation-adjusted 2013 dollars). Or they note that defense spending dwarfs the size of America's diplomatic, foreign assistance, and homeland security spending levels, which total around $100 billion a year between them.[13]

The numbers games go on. Some defense hawks describe the cuts made under President Obama as already totaling $1 trillion over ten years (before sequestration). They make that claim by including cuts made prior to the Budget Control Act of 2011—which were in fact not cuts at all but simply a scaling back of plans for growth that the Pentagon had previously assumed. Some defense budget critics go to the other extreme and claim that there have been no cuts yet, even under the initial effects of the Budget Cointrol Act. This too is misleading. In fact, in 2011, 2012, and 2013, defense budgets exclusive of war costs were effectively held constant relative to the year before, without adjustments for inflation.[14] That amounts to a significant real cut in spending, and one that will not be reversed in future years according to current plans (since the budget will grow roughly with the rate of inflation in those future years, but not much more). Again, it is easy to blow smoke—or at least to confuse—in this business.

In summary, the U.S. defense budget is, and will remain, large relative to the budgets of other countries, and relative to historical precedent. Yet at the same time, it is modest as a fraction of the nation's economy in comparison with the cold war era. That means we need to determine the size of any future defense budget cuts based on careful analysis, not hand waving or ideology.

As a matter of grand strategy, the United States needs to address its weaknesses and strengthen its economic, scientific, and societal foundations of long-term power—without jeopardizing short-term international stability in the process. This may be the simplest way to describe the essence of America's challenge in the current era.

Core Objectives of U.S. Defense Strategy Today

As the United States seeks to cut defense spending, it must have a clear sense of what it would mean to go too far in the venture and scrupulously avoid doing so. Irreducible U.S. defense objectives include limiting the spread of nuclear weapons, protecting the global commons while deterring the rise of powers that might challenge today's generally stable international system, and preventing crises or conflicts from metastasizing into large regional wars in strategically crucial parts of the world. These are high-level, broader goals of grand strategy (as reflected in the National Security Strategy, authored by the White House). At a still greater level of specificity, American military strategy must seek to do the following (and should be reflected in the National Military Strategy, a Pentagon document, as well as the Pentagon's upcoming 2014 Quadrennial Defense Review):

—Responsibly end the nation's current war, with sustained modest commitments to Afghanistan thereafter for what could be an extensive period;

—Deter an assertive Iran in the broader Persian Gulf and Middle East;

—Preserve stability in East Asia in the face of major structural changes due to the rise of China;

—Through exercises, joint planning, integration of forces, and collaboration in missions when they arise, keep a sufficiently robust NATO alliance to provide some basis for global action by a community of democracies, while reducing whatever remote risks remain of Russia again becoming threatening;

—Maintain enough combat capability to wage one substantial, extended regional war in key strategic locations (for example in Korea, even though such a war is quite unlikely), while also carrying out perhaps two smaller operations at the same time;

—Retain a reliable, safe nuclear deterrent that is the equal of Russia's and superior to China's, even as the United States pursues lower force levels through arms control, as well as reasonable capabilities for missile defense;

—Maintain a strong all-volunteer military, with quality of personnel comparable to that of recent years;

—Retain the world's best scientific and defense industrial base; and

—Maintain some capacity to help stop genocide and other mass atrocities as part of a coalition, since America's values are part of what helps it hold together a large network of nations in common strategic cause.

This list seems very extensive, but it has limits. For example, preparing for large-scale war in Europe is no longer necessary even as a remote contingency. The improved European security environment is mostly due to the fact that while Russia is not a completely friendly or benign power, it is not a military threat to the United States or its major allies. Scenarios involving possible Russian attacks on countries like Georgia, as in the 2008 war, are not good candidates for direct American or NATO intervention.[15] The idea of actual war between the United States and Russia is not a reasonable basis for American defense planning. Sanctions and diplomacy are more reasonable and appropriate tools for any future serious disagreements that may occur with Moscow. American conventional force planning has already largely moved beyond contingencies involving Russia, however, so apart from some economies on the nuclear front, this is not an area offering large potential savings.

Others could still argue that the above list of requirements is too long. They might assert, for example, that the United States need not focus as intently on the Middle East as in the past, especially since the boon in North American energy production may make this continent energy-independent within a decade or so. But in addition to the fact that a number of key American friends are found there, the Middle East remains the location of more than a quarter of today's global oil production and more than half of world oil reserves.[16] And the global oil market is interconnected and interdependent. Creative strategies for greater burden-sharing in protecting Gulf oil are appropriate, and are discussed in the pages below; U.S. disengagement from the region is not appropriate.

The rest of this book is an effort to show how the United States can remain resolute and firm in commitment to the above core list of defense priorities while looking to save money in other ways. Some of the recommended approaches would assume a certain amount of increased military risk, to be sure, but the analysis is designed to look for savings that would minimize that risk and keep it within tolerable bounds.

Box 1-1. *American Strategic Assets*

The United States is still the world's top economic power, with more than 19 percent of global gross domestic product (GDP) in 2011 even when purchasing power parity methods are employed.[1]

The United States leads a global alliance system of more than sixty partner states that collectively account for more than 80 percent of total global military spending.[2] That U.S.-led system includes the NATO alliance, bilateral alliances in East Asia and the Western Pacific, the Rio Pact in Latin America, and American security partnerships with Taiwan, Israel, and the Gulf Cooperation Council.

America's nemeses and potential adversaries—Iran, North Korea, Venezuela, Syria, and one or two other such countries—collectively account for 1 to 2 percent of global economic output and a similar fraction of global military power.

U.S. demographics, including its appeal to immigrants and melting-pot traditions, are more favorable than those of almost any other country.[3] Would-be rivals like China, Russia, and India all have far less favorable demographics. The first is afflicted with overpopulation, combined with the resulting one-child policy that promises huge economic challenges within a generation.[4] Russia suffers from underpopulation. India is already hugely challenged by the size of its still-growing population and is hardly an American nemesis in any event.

American universities are still the best in the world. One recent survey estimates that twenty of the world's top fifty institutions of higher learning are on U.S. soil.[5]

Regarding research and development spending, the United States still accounts for nearly one-third of the global total. U.S. spending of $400 billion annually, according to the latest figures, easily outdistances all of Europe combined and is still more than twice the research levels of either China or Japan.[6] Americans no longer obtain the outright majority of world patents, but they do still receive almost half the total despite being only 5 percent of global population.[7]

High-tech American industries like aerospace, pharmaceuticals, and software development remain robust, with the United States typically producing 20 to 50 percent of global output in these areas of innovation and production. Indeed, in the broad category of knowledge- and technology-intensive industry, the United States leads the world—not only in total production but in the percent of its manufacturing output associated with such advanced goods.[8]

The World Economic Forum still rates the United States eighth in the world in overall competitiveness—and second among major, large powers after Germany, with only the small states of Switzerland, Sweden, Singapore, Finland, and the Netherlands outscoring it. By comparison, China comes in at position 29, and Turkey, Brazil, India, and Russia at positions 43, 48, 59, and 67, respectively.[9]

---

1. International Monetary Fund, *World Economic Outlook 2012* (October 2012), p. 179 (www.imf.org/external/ pubs/ft/weo/2012/02/pdf/statapp.pdf).
2. International Institute for Strategic Studies, *The Military Balance 2012* (Oxfordshire, England: Routledge, 2012), pp. 467–73.
3. Joseph S. Nye Jr., *The Future of Power* (New York: Public Affairs, 2011), pp. 189–90.
4. Feng Wang, "China's Population Destiny: The Looming Crisis," Brookings, September 2010 (www.brookings.edu/articles/2010/09_china_population_wang.aspx).
5. *U.S. News and World Report*, "World's Best Universities 2012" (www.usnews.com/education/worlds-best-universities-rankings/top-400-universities-in-the-world?page=3).
6. National Science Board, *Science and Engineering Indicators 2012* (Arlington, Va.: National Science Foundation, 2012) (www.nsf.gov/statistics/seind12/c4/c4s8.htm).
7. Darrell M. West, *Brain Gain* (Brookings, 2010), p. 129.
8. National Science Board, *Science and Engineering Indicators 2012*, chapter 6 (www.nsf.gov/statistics/seind12/c6/c6h.htm).
9. Klaus Schwab, ed., *The Global Competitiveness Report 2012/2013* (Geneva, Switzerland: World Economic Forum, 2012), p. 15 (www.weforum.org/reports/global-competitiveness- report-2012-2013).

Box 1-2. *American Strategic Liabilities*

Prior to the 2011 budget deal between President Barack Obama and Congress (the Budget Control Act), debt held by the public was headed toward 100 percent of GDP and beyond by decade's end—a figure previously experienced only in the 1940s—with long-term budgetary and demographic trends offering no natural respite from this dilemma. Even with sequestration-scale cuts in spending, publicly held debt is expected to remain at its current level of about 75 percent of GDP over the next decade.[1]

The U.S. gross savings rate is now about 13 percent of GDP, just over half the global average. Europe and Japan average closer to 20 percent, and the newly industrializing countries of Asia closer to 30 percent.[2]

Consider traditional manufacturing sectors. As of 2011, China produced 18.4 million motor vehicles, compared to the U.S. total of 8.6 million and Japan's 8.4 million (with Germany fourth at 6.3 million and South Korea fifth at 4.7 million). A decade earlier, it was America in the top spot, making 12.8 million vehicles with Japan second at 10.1 million, Germany third at 5.5 million, France fourth at 3.3 million, and South Korea, Spain, and Canada all ahead of China.[3]

Shipbuilding is now dominated by China as well as South Korea and Japan. The United States barely shows up on global production tables.[4]

Overall manufacturing output as a percent of U.S. GDP declined from 21.2 percent in 1979 to just 11.7 percent three decades later.[5]

The country's overall public school performance is mediocre by global standards. The United States ranks forty-seventh among all countries in secondary school enrollment, forty-seventh in math and science education, twenty-eighth in overall educational quality, and twenty-fourth in Internet access in school, according to the World Economic Forum.[6]

While the World Economic Forum does rate the United States eighth overall in competitiveness, this is despite a number of serious weaknesses. Looking across various subcategories, the Forum rates the United States only 41st in the world in the strength of its institutions, 14th in the quality of its infrastructure, and a remarkably poor 111th in macroeconomic fundamentals.[7]

---

1. Congressional Budget Office, *The Budget and Economic Outlook, Fiscal Years 2013 to 2023*, February 5, 2013, p. 9 (www.cbo.gov/publication/43907).

2. International Monetary Fund, *World Economic Outlook 2012* (October 2012), pp. 216–17 (www.imf.org/external/pubs/ft/weo/2012/01/pdf/text.pdf).

3. International Organization of Motor Vehicle Manufacturers, "Global Vehicle Manufacturing 2000–2011," Paris, France, 2012 (oica.net/category/production-statistics).

4. Shipbuilders' Association of Japan, "Shipbuilding Statistics," March 2010 (www.sajn.or.jp/c/statistics/Shipbuilding_Statistics_Mar2010.pdf).

5. Executive Office of the President, *Economic Report of the President 2012* (Washington, 2012), Table B-12 (www.whitehouse.gov/sites/default/files/microsites/ERP_2012_Complete.pdf).

6. World Economic Forum, *The Global Competitiveness Report 2012–2013* (Geneva, Switzerland, 2012), p. 361.

7. Klaus Schwab, ed., *Global Competitiveness Report 2012/2013* (Geneva, Switzerland: World Economic Forum, 2012), p. 17.

2

ARMY AND MARINE CORPS FORCE STRUCTURE

Today's U.S. Army is slightly larger than half a million soldiers strong, in the active force; the Marine Corps is at 200,000. Both numbers are headed downward, with the Iraq war over and Afghanistan winding down, to current targets of about 490,000 and 182,000, respectively. How much smaller, if any, can they become? And what about the Army reserve component in particular—another half million soldiers in all?

Some historical perspective is in order. In World War II, the United States Army had nearly 6 million personnel on active duty (not counting the Army Air Force or other services).[1] During the Vietnam War, the Army's active-duty forces were almost 1.5 million soldiers strong. Under President Ronald Reagan, the Army active-duty troop figure was more like 800,000. After reducing that strength when the cold war ended to less than half a million, and after considering Donald Rumsfeld's ideas in early 2001 to cut even more, the nation built up its standing Army by almost 100,000 troops over the last decade while also increasing the size of the Marine Corps from about 170,000 to 200,000 active-duty Marines. The

Table 2-1. *U.S. Military Active Duty Personnel, 1960–2012*

	Total	Army	Navy	Marine Corps	Air Force
1960	2,492,037	877,749	624,895	175,919	813,474
1961	2,552,912	893,323	641,995	185,165	832,429
1962	2,687,690	962,712	662,837	192,049	870,092
1963	2,695,240	961,211	668,626	189,937	875,466
1964	2,690,141	972,546	670,160	189,634	857,801
1965	2,723,800	1,002,427	690,162	198,328	832,883
1966	3,229,209	1,310,144	740,646	280,641	897,778
1967	3,411,931	1,468,754	749,299	299,501	894,377
1968	3,489,588	1,516,973	759,163	308,138	905,314
1969	3,449,271	1,514,223	764,867	311,627	858,554
1970	2,983,868	1,293,276	677,152	246,153	767,287
1971	2,626,785	1,050,425	615,767	204,738	755,855
1972	2,356,301	849,824	593,135	199,624	713,718
1973	2,231,908	791,460	566,653	192,064	681,731
1974	2,157,023	784,128	546,464	192,174	634,257
1975	2,104,795	775,301	532,270	195,683	601,541
1976	2,083,581	782,668	527,781	189,851	583,281
1977	2,074,543	782,246	529,895	191,707	570,695
1978	2,062,404	771,624	530,253	190,815	569,712
1979	2,027,494	758,852	523,937	185,250	559,455
1980	2,050,826	777,036	527,352	188,469	557,969
1981	2,082,897	781,473	540,502	190,620	570,302
1982	2,108,612	780,391	552,996	192,380	582,845
1983	2,123,349	779,643	557,573	194,089	592,044
1984	2,138,157	780,180	564,638	196,214	597,125
1985	2,151,032	780,787	570,705	198,025	601,515
1986	2,169,112	780,980	581,119	198,814	608,199
1987	2,174,217	780,815	586,842	199,525	607,035
1988	2,138,213	771,847	592,570	197,350	576,446

continued on next page

ground forces are now headed downward to active-duty strengths that will leave them larger, but only slightly, than their 1990s levels.

The American military today is the second largest in the world, after China's. But it is only modestly larger than those of North Korea, India, and Russia. The size of its active-duty Army also only modestly surpasses those of South Korea and Turkey, among others.

Table 2-1. *U.S. Military Active Duty Personnel, 1960–2012 (Continued)*

	Total	Army	Navy	Marine Corps	Air Force
1989	2,130,229	769,741	592,652	196,956	570,880
1990	2,046,144	732,403	581,856	196,652	535,233
1991	1,986,259	710,821	570,966	194,040	510,432
1992	1,807,177	610,450	541,883	184,529	470,315
1993	1,705,103	572,423	509,950	178,379	444,351
1994	1,610,490	541,343	468,662	174,158	426,327
1995	1,518,224	508,559	434,617	174,639	400,409
1996	1,471,722	491,103	416,735	174,883	389,001
1997	1,438,562	491,707	395,564	173,906	377,385
1998	1,406,830	483,880	382,338	173,142	367,470
1999	1,385,703	479,426	373,046	172,641	360,590
2000	1,384,338	482,170	373,193	173,321	355,654
2001	1,385,116	480,801	377,810	172,934	353,571
2002	1,411,634	486,542	383,108	173,733	368,251
2003	1,434,377	499,301	382,235	177,779	375,062
2004	1,426,836	499,543	373,197	177,480	376,616
2005	1,389,394	492,728	362,941	180,029	353,696
2006	1,384,968	505,402	350,197	180,416	348,953
2007	1,379,551	522,017	337,547	186,492	333,495
2008	1,401,757	543,645	332,228	198,505	327,379
2009	1,418,542	553,044	329,304	202,786	333,408
2010	1,430,985	566,045	328,303	202,441	334,196
2011	1,414,149	558,571	322,629	200,225	332,724
2012	1,388,028	546,057	314,339	198,820	328,812

Source: Department of Defense, Military Personnel Statistics website (http://siadapp. dmdc.osd.mil/personnel/MILITARY/miltop.htm).

Note: Figures are as of September 30 for each year. Numbers do not include activated reservists or full-time employees of the National Guard.

It is important not to latch onto some strategic fad to justify radical cuts in the U.S. Army or Marine Corps. For two decades, since Operation Desert Storm, some have favored "stand-off" warfare featuring long-range strikes from planes and ships as the American military's main approach to future combat. But it is not possible to address many of the world's key security challenges that way—including scenarios in places like Korea and South Asia, discussed further below, that could in fact imperil American security. In the 1990s, advocates of a so-called "military revolution" often argued for such an approach to war. But the subsequent decade proved that even with all the progress in sensors and munitions and other military capabilities, the United States still needed forces on the ground to deal with complex insurgencies and other threats.

A military emphasis on stand-off warfare is sometimes linked with a broader grand strategy of "offshore balancing" by which the distant United States would step in with limited amounts of power to shape overseas events, particularly in Eurasia, rather than getting involved directly with its own soldiers and Marines. But offshore balancing is too clever by half. In fact, overseas developments are not so easily nudged in favorable directions through modest outside interventions. One reason is that offshore balancing can suggest, in the minds of friends and foes alike, a lack of real American commitment. That can embolden adversaries. It can also worry allies to the point where, among other things, they may feel obliged to build up their own nuclear arsenals—as the likes of South Korea, Japan, Taiwan, Turkey, Egypt, and Saudi Arabia might well do absent strong security ties with America. Put plainly, offshore balancing greatly exaggerates American power by assuming that belated and limited uses of U.S. force can swing overseas events in acceptable directions.

Today's Army organizes its forces and measures its strength more commonly in terms of brigades than the old standard of divisions. There are now four brigades to a standard division. The brigades have been turned into units that are independently deployable and operable in the field. Today's ground forces include forty-five brigade combat teams in the active Army and twenty-eight in the National Guard. The Army also has thirteen combat aviation brigades in the active force and eight in the reserve component. The Marines, organized somewhat differently and using different terminology to describe their main formations, have eleven infantry regiments and four artillery regiments (of which nine and three are in the active force, respectively).[2] Roughly speaking, a Marine Corps regiment is comparable in size and capability to an Army brigade.

Throughout the 1990s, U.S. ground forces were sized and shaped primarily to maintain a two-war capability. The wars were assumed to begin in fairly rapid succession (though not exactly simultaneously), and then overlap, lasting several months to perhaps a year or two. Three separate administrations—those of George H. W. Bush, Bill Clinton, and George W. Bush, and a total of five defense secretaries (Richard Cheney, Les Aspin, William Perry, William Cohen, and Donald Rumsfeld)—endorsed some variant of the two-war capability. They formalized the logic in the first Bush administration's 1992 "Base Force" concept, the Clinton administration's 1993 "Bottom-Up Review" followed four years later by the first Quadrennial Defense Review (QDR), and then Secretary Rumsfeld's own 2001 and 2006 QDRs. These reviews all gave considerable attention to both Iraq and North Korea as plausible adversaries. More generally, though, they postulated that the United States could not predict all future enemies or conflicts, and that there was a strong deterrent logic in being able to handle more than one problem at a time. Otherwise, if engaged in a single war in one place, the United States could be vulnerable to opportunistic adversaries elsewhere.[3] This approach clearly could not deter all conflicts; for one thing, having military capability does not always translate into a willingness to use that capability. But in places where American resolve is most manifest, the rationale would seem to be reasonably compelling. While Iraqi dictator Saddam Hussein is gone, and Iraq now poses much less of a direct overland invasion threat to its neighbors and the region, much of this deterrent logic remains valid, though it can now be modified.

The Obama administration appears to agree. Its 2010 *Quadrennial Defense Review* states that after successfully concluding current wars, "in the mid- to long term, U.S. military forces must plan and prepare to prevail in a broad range of operations that may occur in multiple theaters in overlapping time frames. That includes maintaining the ability to prevail against two capable nation-state aggressors. . . ."[4] Still,

Obama scaled back the presumed likelihood of two truly simultaneous large land wars. Indeed, his January 2012 Pentagon guidance places somewhat more limited demands upon U.S. forces, stating that "even when U.S. forces are committed to a large-scale operation in one region, *they will be capable of denying the objectives of—or imposing unacceptable costs on—an opportunistic aggressor in a second region.*"[5] The same review also stated that planning for large-scale stabilization missions would no longer drive the size of U.S. ground forces.

Although the feasibility of ruling out large-scale stabilization missions quite so categorically can be debated, I believe the two-war requirement can be scaled back somewhat further for purposes of force planning. A new ground-force planning paradigm might be termed "one war plus two missions" or "1 + 2." Those missions might, for example, include residual efforts in Afghanistan, contribution to peacekeeping in a place like Congo, or perhaps contribution to a future multilateral stabilization force in Syria or Yemen (even if such missions seem unlikely and undesirable at present). This approach strikes the right balance. It is prudent because it provides some additional capability if and when the nation again engages in a major conflict, and because it provides a bit of a combat cushion should that war go less well than initially hoped. It is modest and economical, however, because it assumes only one such conflict at a time (despite the experience of the last decade) and because it does not envision major ground wars against the world's major overseas powers on their territories.

If a conflict pitted the United States against China, for example, it is reasonable to assume that the fighting would be in maritime and littoral regions. That is because the most plausible threat that China would pose is to Taiwan, or perhaps to neighboring states over disputed sea and seabed resources. Similarly, in regard to possible war against Iran, the most plausible conflict would focus on its nuclear program and waterways in and about the Persian Gulf. Neither of these scenarios would be likely to involve substantial numbers of American ground forces. It is therefore reasonable for the United States to have the capability for just one ground war at a time as long as it can respond in

Figure 2-1. *Number of Active Conflicts Worldwide, 1946–2009*

Number

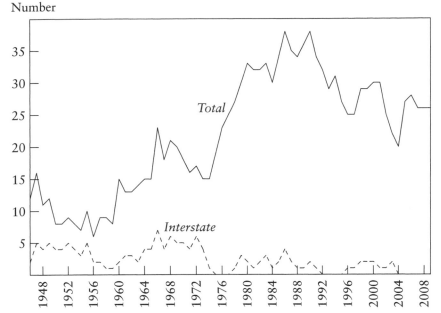

Note: A snapshot on casualties during some of these wars: The Korea conflict of the 1950s left an estimated 2.5+ million dead. In the 1960s, conflicts in Vietnam (1–3 million killed), and Zaire and Nigeria (1–3 million killed) contributed to the totals for the decade. The 1970s brought the Bangladesh Liberation War, which killed between 300,000 and 3 million civilians, as well as Cambodia's civil war (200,000+ killed), Ugandan conflicts that left hundreds of thousands dead, and several wars in the Horn of Africa. Angola (500,000+ killed), Mozambique (1 million+ killed), Afghanistan (1 million+ killed), and conflicts in Central America were among the major wars of the 1980s. The 1990s brought war to Bosnia (100,000 killed), Kosovo (6,000–12,000 killed), Liberia (150,000+ killed), and Sierra Leone (50,000 killed). Thus far in the 2000s, major conflicts include Afghanistan (under 50,000), Iraq (100,000+ killed), Congo (350,000+ killed), and Sudan (200,000+ killed)

Source: Joseph Hewitt, Jonathan Wilkenfeld and Ted Gurr, "Peace and Conflict 2012: Executive Summary," University of Maryland, 2012, p. 18 (www.cidcm.umd.edu/pc/executive _summary/exec_sum_2012.pdf). For Afghanistan in 2000s, see www.brookings.edu/ afghanistanindex.

other ways to other possibly simultaneous and overlapping challenges abroad.

Moreover, the "1 + 2" concept provides some remaining capacity for a small initial response in a second conflict. The forces for the two presumed smaller and less lethal missions could if necessary provide the vanguard of a blocking or emergency response force in the very unlikely event of a second major conflict. And while my option would not increase the size of the Army National Guard, Army Reserve, or Marine Corps Reserve, it would not cut them substantially either—meaning these forces would remain available not only to support active forces in immediate operations but to provide the basis for a rapid increase in active-duty strength through more general mobilization should that be needed.

We should not overestimate the quick-response capabilities of the main combat brigades of the Army National Guard in particular. In the 1980s and 1990s they were perhaps underappreciated; today, because they distinguished themselves in many ways in Iraq and Afghanistan, the risk is that we will forget that it took time for this capability to be honed and we will exaggerate what they can do within a few months of mobilization, early in any future war. But other parts of the reserve component are hugely important and capable, and as a strategic reserve for mobilization purposes, the Army National Guard is too.

Admittedly, despite the hedge provided by the "1 + 2" concept, there is some risk associated with dialing back capabilities in this way, but it would not be radical or unprecedented. During the cold war, American defense posture varied between periods of major ambition—as with the "2½ war" framework of the 1960s that envisioned simultaneous conflicts against the Soviet Union (probably in Europe), China in East Asia, and some smaller foe elsewhere—and somewhat more realistic approaches, as under Richard Nixon, which dropped the requirement to 1½ wars. Nixon's "1 war" would have been conflict in Europe against the Warsaw Pact, a threat that is now gone. His regional war capability, or his "1/2 war" posture, was therefore similar to what I am proposing here.[6]

To compensate for its modest size, this one-war combat capability needs to be responsive and highly effective. That fact has implications in areas like strategic transport, which must not be reduced. It also has implications for the National Guard and Reserves, which remain indispensable parts of the total force. They have done well in Iraq and Afghanistan and merit substantial support in the years ahead—better than they have often received in our nation's past.[7] But they are not able to carry out prompt deployments to crises or conflicts in the way that current American security commitments and current deterrence strategy require. As such, we should not move to a "citizens army" that depends primarily on reservists for the nation's defense.

What does the 1 + 2 framework mean for sizing the Army and Marine Corps? It should allow for roughly 15 percent cutbacks relative to recent peak levels. Army active-duty brigade combat teams might number about thirty-eight, with the National Guard adding twenty-four more. (Alternatively, the Army may wind up with less than thirty-eight if it adds a third maneuver battalion to each.) Combat aviation units might decline to eleven and seven brigades in the active and National Guard forces, respectively.

The Marines would give up two major units, resulting in ten infantry and three artillery regiments in their active forces, while keeping their three divisions and three associated Marine Expeditionary Forces.

The resulting combined ground force would be enough to sustain about twenty combat brigades overseas indefinitely, and to surge to twenty-five to thirty if need be.

This force-sizing math is based on the principle that active forces should have roughly twice as much time at home as on deployment and that reservists should have five times as much time at home as abroad. That would allow enough military capacity for the main invasion phase of the kinds of wars assumed throughout 1990s defense planning and the invasion of Iraq actually carried out in 2003; force packages ranging from fifteen to twenty brigades were generally assumed or used for these missions.[8]

The capacity outlined above falls short of the twenty-two brigades deployed in 2007/2008 just to Iraq and Afghanistan. If long crises or conflicts occurred in the future, therefore, we would have to ratchet force strength back up. The Army and Marine Corps of the last ten years have, fortunately, already proven they can do this. They added 15 percent in new capability within about half a decade without any reduction in the excellence of individual units.

Some might question whether we even still need a one-war capability. But it is not hard to imagine plausible scenarios. Even if each specific case is unlikely, a number of scenarios cannot be ruled out.[9]

Consider a possible contingency on the Korean peninsula. This would not necessarily result from the traditional scenario of an invasion of South Korea by the North. It could be sparked, rather, by an internal coup or schism within North Korea that destabilized the country and put the security of its nuclear weapons at risk. It also could result, somewhat inadvertently, from an exchange of gunfire on land or sea that escalated into North Korean long-range artillery and missile attacks on South Korea's nearby capital of Seoul. The North Korean aggressions of 2010, including the brazen sinking of the South Korean Navy ship *Cheonan* and subsequent attacks on a remote South Korean island that together killed about 50 South Koreans, are instructive here.[10]

Alternatively, if North Korea greatly accelerated its production of nuclear bombs—it is now believed to have about eight—or seemed on the verge of selling nuclear materials to a terrorist group, the United States and South Korea might decide to preempt with a limited strike against its nuclear facilities. North Korea might then respond in dramatic fashion.

The allies would surely defeat North Korea in any war and then quite probably occupy the country and change its government. North Korea's weaponry is more obsolescent than ever, it faces major fuel and spare parts shortages in training and preparing its forces, and its personnel are undernourished and otherwise underprepared.[11] Yet North Korea has a million-man army, as well as a very large reserve. All these soldiers can be assumed to have workable small arms. The nature of the terrain in Korea means that much of the battle would ultimately be infantry combat. North Korean soldiers are still indoctrinated with the notion that they must defend their homeland at all costs. For a half-century, North Korea has built up fortifications near the DMZ that could make the task of extricating its forces difficult and bloody. North Korea also has among the world's largest artillery concentrations and could conduct intense shelling of Seoul in any war from positions that its forces already occupy.

Even the potential for nuclear attacks by the North against South Korean, Japanese, or American assets cannot be dismissed. Attempts at outright annihilation of Seoul or Tokyo would make little sense, as allied forces could respond in kind and would surely track down the perpetrators of such a heinous crime. Any North Korean nuclear attack on a major allied city would mean overthrow of the Pyongyang regime and almost surely death (or at least lifetime imprisonment) for its leaders once they were found. But Pyongyang might try more limited actions. Perhaps it would try to use one nuclear bomb, out of its presumed arsenal of eight or so, against a remote airbase or troop concentration. This could weaken allied defenses in a key sector while also signaling the North's willingness to escalate further if necessary. It would be a hugely risky move but is not totally inconceivable given previous North Korean actions.

Possible Chinese intervention would have to be guarded against, as well. Beijing would probably not be eager to come to the armed defense of the most fanatical military dictatorship left on earth. But it also has treaty obligations with the North that may complicate its calculations. And it would be worried about any possibility of American encroachment into North Korean lands near its borders. It might seek to preempt that possibility by moving its own forces into northern North Korea to establish a buffer zone. For all these reasons, a Korean war could have broader regional implications. This requires that Washington and Seoul maintain close consultations with Beijing in any future crisis or conflict and perhaps find ways to anticipate or even welcome a possible limited Chinese military role in such a scenario. But it also suggests that U.S. and South Korean forces would want to have the capability to win any war against the North quickly and decisively, before Seoul was destroyed or nuclear weapons used or nuclear materials smuggled out of the country, for example. Moving fast would also reduce the odds that China would decide to establish an overly large buffer zone in an anarchic North Korea with its own forces in a way that could bring Chinese and allied soldiers into close proximity.

Chances are that none of the above will happen, precisely because North Korea knows what the consequences would be. This is an argument for making cuts carefully and retaining American engagement in Korea. Deterrence is working. American strategy on balance is successful there and elsewhere in keeping the peace, and the United States must not lose sight of this key reality in its efforts to cut the deficit. Modest defense cuts may be sensible; radical changes should be considered with great skepticism given the ongoing threats of today's international environment.

To sustain deterrence, U.S. forces available for Korea—in addition to the 30,000 now stationed there—should remain quite substantial. They might focus largely on air and naval capabilities, given South Korea's large and improved army. But they should also involve American ground forces, since a speedy victory would be of the essence, and since as noted the fighting could be quite difficult and manpower requirements intensive. Some have argued that, given the mathematical requirements of a stabilization mission in a country of some 24 million, South Korea's army could in principle handle much of the stabilization task itself, since it could generate up to 400,000 soldiers.[12] But that perspective overlooks the potential challenges of defeating North Korea's army militarily on such complex terrain in a serious fight—in contrast to the requirements of a more benign stabilization mission. Deterrence also works better when leaders in Pyongyang cannot persuade themselves that South Korea could somehow be intimidated into a coerced compromise if it was abandoned by erstwhile allies. For all these reasons, being able to bring several U.S. divisions to bear makes eminent military sense.

American ground forces would also be important because American mobile assets (such as the 101st air assault division and Marine amphibious forces) provide capabilities that South Korea does not itself possess in comparable numbers. These U.S. forces could, among other things, help seal North Korean borders so nuclear materials could not be smuggled out. Perhaps fifteen to twenty brigade-sized forces and eight to ten fighter wings, as well as three to four carrier battle groups, would be employed by the United States, as all previous defense reviews of the post–cold war era have rightly concluded. American forces might not be needed long in any occupation of the North, given South Korea's large capabilities, but they could be crucial for a few months.

Standing U.S. ground forces that were 15 percent smaller than today's could handle the above. They would also provide options for other remote, yet hardly inconceivable, scenarios. For example, they would retain the ability to overthrow a regime such as that in Teheran that carried out a heinous act of aggression or terror against American interests.[13] That type of operation is highly improbable, and would be extraordinarily difficult—but the capability to conduct it, in extremis, could be a deterrent. (Such a capability could also be useful against any other powerful extremist government with ties to terrorists and nuclear ambitions or capabilities.) Overthrowing Iran's government and leaving the country in chaos would hardly be an ideal outcome. But the prospect could nonetheless be a meaningful deterrent against Iranian extremism, as the United States could, if absolutely necessary, defeat and largely destroy the Revolutionary Guard and Qods forces that keep the current extremists in power. The aggregate size, combat capability, divisional force structure, combat aircraft inventories, and other such capabilities of the Iranian forces are broadly consistent with those of the nominal regional foe that has focused American defense planning for two decades.[14] These facts suggest that what has been viewed as a "one regional war" American force package would likely be adequate to defeat and/or largely destroy the Iranian military.

To the extent that the international community as a whole then saw the reestablishment of order in Iran as important, U.S. allies could, if desired, help provide ground forces in a subsequent coalition to stabilize the country—a job that could require half a million troops. (Even today's American ground forces would in fact be inadequate to the job of stabilizing Iran, which with 80 million people is three times as populous as either Iraq or Afghanistan.) Other ground combat scenarios against Iran can be imagined too, if for example Iran retaliates against a U.S. or Israeli air strike by invading a neighbor—an unlikely but also hardly unthinkable contingency.[15]

Another quite worrisome scenario could involve a new Indo-Pakistani crisis leading to war between the two nuclear-armed states over Kashmir. This could result, for example, if a more extremist civilian or military leader came to power in Pakistan. As my colleagues Bruce Riedel, Stephen Cohen, and Strobe Talbott have shown, it is quite feasible to see how such an extremist state could take South Asia to the brink of nuclear war by provoking conflict with India. Were that to happen, and perhaps a nuke or two even detonated above an airbase or other such military facility, the world could be faced with the specter of all-out nuclear war in the most densely populated part of the planet.

While hostilities continued, even if the United States would probably avoid taking sides on the ground, Washington might want the option to help India protect itself from missile strikes by Pakistan. It is even possible that the United States might, depending on how the conflict began, consider trying to shoot down *any* missile launched from *either* side at the other, given the huge human and strategic perils associated with nuclear-armed missiles striking the great cities of South Asia.

It is also imaginable that if such a war began and international negotiators were trying to figure out how to end it, an international force could be considered to help implement a cease-fire accord in Kashmir for a number of years. India would be adamantly against this idea today, but things could change if war broke out and such a force seemed the only way to reverse the momentum toward all-out nuclear war in South Asia. American forces would quite likely need to play a key role, since other countries do not have the capacity or political confidence to handle the mission on their own.[16]

With forty-eight brigade equivalents in its active Army and Marine Corps forces, and another twenty-four Army National Guard brigades, the United States could handle a combination of challenges reasonably well. Suppose, for example, that in 2015 the United States had two brigades in a stabilization mission in Yemen and two brigades still in

Afghanistan. Imagine that another war in Korea broke out, requiring a peak of twenty U.S. combat brigades for the first three months, after which fifteen were needed for another year or more. That would be within the capacity of the smaller force.

What is the presumed role of U.S. allies in all of the above? And is it possible to encourage them to do more in the future? Some have understandably raised this question at a time when the United States outspends its allies on defense by a wide margin, not only in terms of actual dollars but in terms of the percentage of GDP devoted to the military. Hans Binnendijk, for example, proposes a concept of "forward partnering."

The fact that America has so many allies is extremely important—it signals that most other major powers around the world are at least loosely aligned with America on major strategic matters. They may not choose to be with the United States on every mission, as the Iraq experience proves. But when America is directly threatened, as with 9/11, the Western alliance system is rather extraordinary. This has been evidenced in Afghanistan where, even beyond the ten-year mark of the war, the coalition still includes combat forces from some forty-eight countries.

How much help do these allies tend to provide? Here the answer is, and will remain, more nuanced. The other forty-seven nations in Afghanistan, at the mission's peak size in 2011, collectively provided fewer than one-third of all foreign forces; the United States by itself provided more than two-thirds. Still, a peak of more than 40,000 non-Afghan forces from countries besides the United States is nothing to trivialize.

The allies took the lead in Libya in 2011. But this may be the exception that proves the rule—the mission that the Europeans led was a very limited air campaign in a nearby country. The French also helped depose a brutal dictator in their former colony of the Ivory Coast in 2011, and as of this writing they are attempting militarily to stabilize northern Mali, though with uncertain prospects at present. These operations have on balance been courageous, and somewhat effective, but limited in scope and size. Some European and Asian allies, as well as other nations, continue to slog away in UN peacekeeping operations in places such as Congo and Lebanon. The Australians tend to be dependable partners; Canada did a great deal in Afghanistan and took heavy losses before finally pulling out its combat forces in 2011. In Asia, the Japanese are also showing some greater assertiveness as their concerns about China's rise lead to more muscular naval operations by Tokyo.

Still, the allies are not stepping up their overall defense efforts, and they almost surely will not in the future. Any hope that the election of Barack Obama with his more inclusive and multilateral style of leadership would lead them to do so are proving generally unwarranted. NATO defense spending is slipping downward, from a starting point that was not very impressive. American allies were collectively more capable in the 1990s, when they contributed most of the ground troops that NATO deployed to the Balkans, than today.

The fraction of GDP that the NATO allies spend on their armed forces had declined to about 1.5 percent by 2012, well under half the U.S. figure. That compares to NATO's average level of 2.2 percent in 2000 and about 2.5 percent in 1990.[17] Before he left office in 2011, Secretary of Defense Robert Gates accordingly warned of the possibility of a two-tier alliance.[18]

When allies feel directly threatened, as Japan and South Korea sometimes do now, they will contribute. South Korea in particular can be counted on to provide many air and naval forces, and most of the needed ground forces, for any major operation on the peninsula in the future. (South Korea is generally, and understandably, less enthusiastic about being pulled into an anti-China coalition.)[19] Taiwan would surely do what it could to help fend off a possible Chinese attack, not leaving the whole job to the American military in the event that terrible scenario someday unfolded (though in terms of preparation, its $10 billion annual budget pales compared to China's and has dropped to just over 2 percent of GDP).[20] Many if not most NATO forces will be careful in drawing down troops from Afghanistan, making cuts roughly in proportion with those of the United States over the next two years.

In the Persian Gulf, both Saudi Arabia and the United Arab Emirates have impressive air forces, each with at least 100 top-of-the-line aircraft, many of them procured from the United States. Both countries certainly could help provide patrols over their own airspace as defensive measures in a future conflict. If they had already been directly attacked by Iran, they might also be willing to carry out counterstrikes against Iranian land or sea targets. But again there are limits. If Iran had not actually attacked their territories, Saudi Arabia and the UAE might prefer to avoid striking Iran themselves first—since once the hostilities ended, they would have to coexist in the same neighborhood. For that and other reasons, it is not completely clear that the United States could count on regional allies to do more than the very important but still limited task of protecting their own airspace. Washington could hope for more but should not count on it for force-planning purposes.

Britain can probably be counted on for a brigade or two—up to 10,000 troops, perhaps, as in Afghanistan—for most major operations that the United States might consider in the future.[21] Some new NATO allies like Poland and Romania, and some potential aspirants like Georgia, will try to help where they can, largely to solidify ties to America that they consider crucial for their security. The allies also *may* have enough collective capacity, and political will, to share responsibility for humanitarian and peace operations in the future. However, the record of the entire Western world, including the United States, is patchy at best on that front. Numerous countries will contribute modestly to limited and low-risk missions like the counterpiracy patrols off the coast of Somalia. If future naval operations are needed to monitor or enforce future sanctions on Iran, Washington may get a few allies to participate. But that is about as far as most allies will go.

The United States need not, and should not, accept primary responsibility for future military operations of a peacekeeping or humanitarian character. But in terms of planning for major war, it will have to assume that its forces—together with those of directly threatened allies—will provide the preponderance of future capability. In specific cases, Washington can always hope for more help. But for planning purposes, it should not count on it. This fact is regrettable at one level. But America should be careful to avoid making the perfect the enemy of the good. The United States leads the greatest alliance system in history, and that fundamental reality is a huge strategic asset that Washington should not jeopardize with unrealistic demands on its security partners. Nor should the United States take a grand strategic gamble of unilateral retrenchment in the hope that such a pullback will produce desirable reactions in key overseas theaters.

3

AIR FORCE AND NAVY
FORCE STRUCTURE

With its rebalancing to Asia as well as the new defense guidance, issued by the Pentagon in early 2012, that envisions avoiding large-scale stabilization missions, such as Afghanistan, in the future, some of the center of gravity of U.S. defense planning is shifting to the Navy and Air Force.

This trend is most evident in the new "AirSea Battle" concept being touted by the two services. The concept emphasizes maintaining access to the global commons, and defense of overseas allies and interests, in light of the spread of advanced technologies (like antiship missiles) as well as the challenges posed by Iran and by China's rise. It seeks to make use of new technologies to counter these perceived trends, which American strategists often summarize as a growing "anti-access/area denial" (or A2AD) capability on the part of potential U.S. foes.[1] AirSea Battle doctrine emphasizes improved command and control, precision strike, advanced defenses, robotics, and networked operations from the subsurface activities of submarines up to the flights of aircraft and the orbits of satellites.

Yet such technological innovations are occurring at a time when any shifts in budgetary resources toward the Air Force and Navy are modest at best. For example, the U.S. Navy is currently maintaining a robust global presence with only about 286 major warships. That is a formidable force of generally high-technology and large vessels, including 11 large-deck aircraft carriers, 11 large amphibious ships with Marine Corps aerial capability, and more than 50 state-of-the-art nuclear-powered attack submarines.[2] But this fleet is only half the size of the Navy's peak under Ronald Reagan. Even with fewer ships, the Navy is maintaining 15 percent more overseas deployment time than it did a decade ago, just before 9/11. The Navy needs to think about new responsibilities too, such as the increasingly ice-free and thus navigable Arctic.[3] For these reasons, the Navy would prefer to expand the fleet. For example, toward the end of his tenure as chief of naval operations in 2011, Admiral Gary Roughead advocated a fleet of 313 ships.[4] The Navy has subsequently recognized that the fleet will not grow so much, given budget constraints, and has revised its goal modestly to 306 ships.[5] My own views, discussed further below, are that in fact modest further reductions in fleet size should be possible.

The Air Force also has assets that are part of America's prompt global-reach capabilities. Chief long-range strike assets feature the Air Force's bombers—sixty-five B-1, twenty B-2, and ninety-four B-52 aircraft. These bombers, as well as transport planes, tactical aircraft, and support aircraft for purposes such as intelligence, make use of roughly 60 KC-10 aerial refueling tankers as well as nearly 200 KC-135 tanker aircraft. Another 300-plus KC-135s are in the Air Reserves and Air National Guard.

These tankers, combined with America's dispersed base network, also allow tactical combat aircraft to be deployed quickly, assuming bases can be found for them in the region of operation. The U.S. Air Force has 1,700 such combat aircraft in its active-duty inventory. The planes can deploy within days if they have somewhere to operate once reaching their destination. The main Air Force combat force structure includes six air superiority wing-equivalents, ten to eleven theater strike wing equivalents, and eight intelligence/reconnaissance wing equivalents, as well as three command and control wings. (The air superiority and strike wings have seventy-two primary planes each; the intelligence wings about forty-five each.) The Air Force also seeks to have the capacity to sustain sixty-five unmanned aerial vehicles on orbit by 2015.[6]

Both the Navy and Air Force have been streamlining over the last decade, even as the Army and Marine Corps have grown. But in fact, further economies are possible. Two main ideas are considered here. The first is a change in how the Navy operates. The second involves relying a bit more on the Air Force, and a bit less on the Navy, for daily vigilance in and around the Persian Gulf.

Sea Swaps and Forward Homeports

In the modern era, the U.S. Navy has wished to sustain major deployments continuously in the Mediterranean, Persian Gulf area, and Western Pacific. Since the cold war ended, the Mediterranean has been deemphasized to a degree, but the Persian Gulf area has received even more attention than before, with no sign of that abating despite the overthrow of Iraqi dictator Saddam Hussein and the departure of most U.S. forces from Iraq.

In the first decade after the cold war, the Navy undertook several innovations. It based some specialty ships like minesweepers overseas, rotating crews by airplane to allow sailors a break without having to waste time bringing the ships home. It also chose to tolerate gaps in naval presence in some theaters, instead "surging" forces at unpredictable times and places. Where some degree of steady presence was viewed as necessary, the Navy would sometimes provide that capability with smaller surface ships or large-deck amphibious vessels rather than aircraft carriers. Building on the practice of overseas homeporting of minesweepers, it also looked into bigger changes in how it deployed ships abroad, as with the so-called Horizon Concept that is related to sea swap as described below.[7]

Table 3-1. *Age of Active Duty Aircraft of the U.S. Air Force Fleet, as of September 30, 2011*

Number of aircraft

Type	Age in years									Total	Average
	0–3	3–6	6–9	9–12	12–15	15–18	18–21	21–24	24+		
A-10									191	191	29.4
B-1								52	14	66	23.8
B-2					2	12	5	1		20	16.8
B-52									58	58	50.4
C-5								20	16	36	30.3
(K)C-10								3	56	59	26.3
C-12	34	2	3	3				4	18	64	15.3
C-17	33	31	37	36	21	16	8			182	8.1
C-20						2		1	8	11	22.8
C-21									26	26	26.3
(V)C-25							1	1		2	20.5
C-32					4					4	12.5
C-37	2	1		7	2					12	5.8
C-40			4							4	6.6
C-130	24	13	4	4	4	15			184	247	27.0
C-135									197	197	49.6
CV-22	12	5	2							19	2.5
E-3									32	32	32.0
E-4									4	4	37.2
E-9A								2		2	19.0

Aircraft										Total	%
F-15C-D							14	106		120	27.7
F-15E	9	14	3	9	90	96				221	19.1
F-16	3	22	7	84	163	122	182			583	20.8
F-22	54	71	32	4						161	3.8
F-35	7	4								11	1.1
H-1								82		82	39.1
H-60	2			6	25	27	9			69	20.5
MQ-1	57	31	22	21	2					133	4.5
MQ-9	50	17	4							71	1.9
RQ-4	13	10	2							25	3.8
T-1				25	105	49				178	16.5
T-6	90	137	142	80	1					450	5.6
T-38								521		521	45.1
T-41							4			4	41.5
T-51		3								3	6.0
U-2					5		27			32	28.0
UV-18			1				2			3	27.3
Gliders	15	15	1							31	9.3
Total	378	322	282	206	77	243	341	408	1,677	3,934	20.4
Percent of total	9.6	8.2	7.2	5.2	2.0	6.2	8.7	10.4	42.6		

Note: In 2007 there were 4,282 aircraft in the active-duty U.S. Air Force inventory; in 2002 there were 4,338; and in 1997 there were 4,496. Additionally, the following portions of the fleet were aged fifteen years or older: 2012 (68 percent); 2007 (70 percent); 2002 (62 percent); 1997 (50 percent).

Sources: 1997 USAF Almanac (May 1997), p. 49; 2002 USAF Almanac (May 2002), p. 58; 2007 USAF Almanac (May 2007), p. 63; 2012 USAF Almanac (May 2012), p. 53 (www.airforce-magazine.com/Almanacs/Pages/USAF Almanacs.aspx).

However, while crews are rotated with minesweepers, a handful of coastal patrol craft, and (as has long been the case) the ballistic missile submarine force, the practice has not been extended to other ships. Experiments have been done with larger vessels, but the Navy has not chosen to adopt the crew-rotation practice for them. This means that a typical surface combatant, like a cruiser or destroyer, spends about six months in home port training for a deployment, then sails for a six-month mission abroad but consumes perhaps two of those months in transit, and then spends another period of at least six months back in home port for recovery and maintenance and other such activities. The net effect is four months on station out of every 18- to 24-month period, a very inefficient ratio.

There is an alternative, one that undoubtedly would be challenging to adopt in some ways—but it is time to work through the challenges and make it happen. By keeping a given ship abroad for roughly two years and having two or three crews share that vessel overseas as well as training ships at home, the Navy can do more with less. In fact, it can improve its deployment efficiency by up to 40 percent per ship, accomplishing with about three-and-a-half ships, on average, what previously might have required five. Focusing on the Navy's large surface combatants—cruisers and destroyers—this approach could theoretically allow roughly fifty-four ships to maintain the global presence that the Navy says it needs—about twenty-one of these ships deployed abroad at a time—rather than the target of eighty-eight ships it currently is pursuing.[8] In other words, the fleet could decline in size by slightly more than a third. This would permit a slowdown in the production of large surface combatants.

For reasons of practical logistics, and reasons of warfighting as discussed below, it would be too much to reduce the Navy by the full total of thirty-four ships implied by the above figures. But reductions of roughly half that magnitude should be feasible. Since the average construction cost of these ships is currently $1.5 billion to $2 billion each, and since operating savings also are possible, net savings could approach $2 billion a year.[9]

This new system of crew rotation would take time to implement, however, and savings would therefore be less over the next ten years than one might estimate at first blush. New practices would have to be worked out, and access to overseas port facilities expanded for routine sustenance and maintenance functions.[10] The Navy is already seeing higher maintenance deficits, due to strain on equipment, and cannot implement such a new approach until it has facilities abroad that can keep its fleet shipshape.[11] Perhaps small bridging teams would have to be kept on board any given ship as one crew departed and another arrived, as well. Undoubtedly, new patterns of communications would need to be established among the officers and top enlisted personnel who were responsible for the transition on a given ship, so that the inevitable glitches could be worked through.

An additional way to get more out of a smaller fleet is to homeport more ships near the theaters where they operate, which helps reduce time wasted in transit. Indeed, about a decade ago, the Navy started down this path in another important way, basing attack submarines on Guam.[12] But the Navy can go well beyond the idea of stationing six submarines there; in fact, there is room to add at least five more. The average number of mission days for a submarine stationed on Guam might be about 100 a year, roughly three times what a submarine stationed in the continental United States can muster. Adding five more submarines to Guam would, in theory, allow a reduction of up to ten attack submarines in the fleet. In practice, to keep an attrition reserve, reducing by five submarines would be more prudent, with annual average savings of something approaching $1 billion.[13]

The Persian Gulf: Land-Based Aircraft versus Navy Presence

One other way to move toward a smaller Navy, without requiring increases in the size of other parts of the U.S. military, concerns foreign basing of military assets in the Persian Gulf region. For years, all the movement has been in favor of reducing U.S. forces in the region. Also, the fact that it costs the Pentagon, on average, $1 million per year to station a single service member in Afghanistan leads many to assume that basing American military personnel abroad, while strategically necessary at times, is generally a bad economy. This logic is flawed.

In fact, there are times when basing American forces abroad saves huge amounts of money—not only because deterrence is cheaper than war, but also because accomplishing a given military task can often be done much more efficiently with forward-stationed units. A case in point today is our ability to maintain tactical combat airpower in the broader Persian Gulf region. At present the United States relies almost exclusively on aircraft carriers, each carrying about seventy-two aircraft, to maintain short-range jets in position for possible conflict with Iran in particular. Over the past decade, however, several squadrons of land-based jets in Saudi Arabia, Kuwait, and Iraq have largely come home.[14] While the United States occasionally rotates fighter jets through the small states of the Gulf Cooperation Council (GCC), and while it maintains command and control and support assets in states like Qatar and the United Arab Emirates, its permanent ashore combat power is very limited.

As a general rule, whenever the United States predictably needs continuous airpower capability in a given region, military logic advocates providing much of it with land-based Air Force (or Marine Corps) assets rather than with aircraft carriers. The reasoning begins with the fact that even a major, hardened land base costs perhaps one-tenth as much as a $12 billion aircraft carrier (not to mention accompanying support ships). But the arithmetic is even more heavily weighted against aircraft carriers in such situations, even if they are obviously still crucial for possible conflict in places where the United States cannot predict future needs. That is because it can take five or six ships of a given type in the fleet to maintain one continuous overseas patrol.

The reason that the United States maintains one or two carriers near the Gulf at a time, rather than relying on land-based jets, has important historical, political, and diplomatic roots. Over the years, the region's governments have wanted to limit their visible association with the United States, and Washington has wanted to keep a distance from regimes seen as anti-Israeli or autocratic or otherwise unpalatable. But in light of Iran's ongoing provocations and its nuclear programs, this past tendency requires rethinking. This is a good example of where greater allied burden-sharing of a certain type may be realistic, given that regional states themselves see a clear threat from Iran, a threat that has grown with time.

It would be a mistake to put all of our eggs in one basket in the Gulf. Given the political sensitivities and uncertainties noted above, it would make the most sense to seek two or even three land bases in different countries in the region, each of which could normally host around fifty American combat jets like the F-15, F-16, or even the stealthy F-22 fighter (and some day the F-35 joint strike fighter, once it is available in adequate numbers). Investment costs for underground fuel lines, hardened aircraft shelters, and the like would ideally be paid largely by the GCC governments.

It is true that Washington must request permission from local governments before employing locally based aircraft in any preemptive strike (with or without Israeli participation) on Iran's nuclear facilities. Getting such permission could be problematic; for example, Saudi Arabia did not allow the United States to conduct aircraft sorties from its bases during the 2003 invasion of Iraq. Some would cite this fact to argue against land-basing. But in fact, Washington could always surge a carrier or two to the region for a strike that occurred at a time of its choosing. The land-based jets would not need to be the vanguard of this operation. It is also worth bearing in mind that while the Saudis, in particular, were of two minds about the overthrow of Saddam, fearing the prospect of a Shia-majority government that would likely succeed him, they have little such ambivalence about the need to remain resolute in dealing with Iran.

This option would take time to implement, so it would not be achievable before 2014 or 2015, when any immediate decisions on striking Iran would have probably been made. So it need not dramatically change the course of current coercive diplomacy toward Iran over its nuclear program.

With this idea, the U.S. aircraft carrier fleet might eventually be reduced from eleven ships to nine, with an estimated average savings in the defense budget approaching $10 billion a year.[15] Indeed, given ship maintenance schedules, the Navy is already going to operate a fleet with only nine available carriers in the coming years, so this option simply would make a virtue out of necessity, at least in the short term.[16] At a minimum, it is an idea to discuss intensively with key allied governments in the Gulf region.

On balance, the Navy does not need to add 10 percent more vessels to its force structure to carry out current practices and presence. Indeed, it can do well with 10 percent less, or about 260 major ships.

The Air Force also can make do with a somewhat smaller force structure. Its current combined number of tactical combat wing equivalents, seventeen, is probably excessive in light of several trends. First, the quality of the F-22 and F-35 aircraft is extraordinary, as is the quality of the precision munitions that have come to dominate modern warfare. The idea that roughly ten tactical fighter wings were needed for a given regional conflict took root twenty years ago, when aircraft as advanced as the F-22 and F-35 were not a significant part of the force and when precision munitions typically represented 10 percent of the amount of ordnance dropped (in contrast to closer to 80–90 percent today). Precision-guided munitions have a roughly tenfold greater effectiveness against most targets than do unguided weapons,[17] yet wings with fifth-generation aircraft will have at least 85 percent as many jets as earlier units.

In addition, Marine Corps combat aircraft have not been adequately considered in previous planning. These are admittedly designed more for use in support of ground forces. But with the lower risk of simultaneous ground combat operations in the modern era, and with the greater interservice cooperation or "jointness" now typical of modern air operations, this assumption can be modified and Marine Corps aircraft can contribute more to roles assigned previously to the Air Force and Navy. Thus, even with this greater reliance on forward-deployed Air Force capability in the Persian Gulf, Air Force tactical combat capability can be reduced from seventeen to fifteen wing equivalents.

Testing the Smaller Navy against Plausible Warfighting Needs

If, as I have suggested, the Navy and Air Force can save money by shifting how they maintain normal presence, the question arises: How well would the smaller Navy and Air Force, and new operational and basing practices, work for wartime scenarios?

A difficult test of the future Navy would be countering a protracted Chinese effort to blockade Taiwan. This is a very unlikely and undesirable scenario; yet it is still plausible, and as such is important to consider for deterrence. The 1979 Taiwan Relations Act states that any attempt to change the status of Taiwan by other than peaceful means would be of "grave concern" to the United States; that is short of a defense treaty commitment to defend Taiwan under all circumstances but does create something of a moral and political commitment.

Beijing's idea in such a situation might be to use a combination of missile strikes against ports, cyberattacks, and ultimately submarines shooting torpedoes or antiship missiles at cargo ships to complicate the ability of any company or foreign entity to trade with Taiwan. By sinking just a single ship and introducing major danger into the voyages of others, China might effectively start to strangle the Taiwanese economy at relatively low risk to itself and at low cost in lives. China could even try to rescue seamen from the ships it attacked to limit the risk of international retribution. Such a scenario would be far more promising for Beijing than an all-out attack and yet potentially almost as effective in cowing Taipei. China might further hope that its antiship capabilities would deter American involvement.

In previous work, I have estimated what the United States might need to do in response, working with Taiwan's military to protect sea and air lanes so that normal commerce could resume. The United States might need a force of up to four aircraft carrier battle groups, reinforced tactical combat airpower on Okinawa and perhaps also the Philippines, and a range of other assets including attack submarines and maritime patrol aircraft. Patrol aircraft would be especially important since China might start attacking American satellites in low-Earth orbit in this kind of engagement. Moreover, I estimated that perhaps 10 to 25 percent of deployed American assets could be lost in such a campaign. In addition, the scenario could last long enough that a "rotation base" would be needed to allow forces to go home periodically for a rest and for equipment maintenance, with fresh units being deployed as required.[18]

All told, in a worst case, this scenario could require the entire recommended U.S. fleet of nine aircraft carriers if it lasted long enough and led to damage or attrition of one or two of them. That is a worst case assessment, and if it happened, Washington could probably find ways to get by without carriers in the Persian Gulf through the use of more land-based airpower. But it is the kind of consideration that underscores the importance of not cutting existing capabilities too deeply.

Scenario analysis is of course always dependent on the specific conditions assumed. But a stress test of the somewhat smaller force I am suggesting shows that it can indeed handle most plausible peacetime, crisis, and combat demands that would be placed upon it. As argued here, it would be feasible to conduct an operation to break a blockade of Taiwan, and as argued in chapter 2, the recommended force would suffice for war in Korea, too (although perhaps not simultaneously), or for a mission against Iran. Washington can find clever ways to sustain capabilities in the Persian Gulf and western Pacific even with a smaller military—if cuts are made carefully and new operational practices adopted.

4

MODERNIZATION

Even after the cuts in planned weapons buys of recent years, it is still the case that we can rethink a number of weapons programs. Some weapons are bought partly out of bureaucratic inertia as well as logrolling by Congress. Some are simply unnecessary or, to be more precise, not worth the money even if they do provide certain attractive capabilities. As Admiral Gary Roughead and Kori Schake have argued, the services continue to add new performance requirements to weapons systems too far into the acquisition process.

The so-called acquisition accounts—primarily research, development, testing, and evaluation (RDT&E) on the one hand, and procurement on the other—together cost the nation almost $200 billion a year in the core defense budget. This is more than China spends on all accounts for its entire military and is at least three times what China spends just on military modernization. All other countries are even further behind. It is also true that the Pentagon has close to a trillion dollars worth of plans on the books just for major weapons systems in the years ahead, completing development and production of weapons it already has in the pipeline.

Yet these acquisition costs represent less than 40 percent of the $550 billion or so in core defense spending. As such, we have to avoid the common mistake of thinking that the best and easiest way to cut the defense budget is always to cut acquisition programs.[1]

Moreover, for all the stories of expensive weapons, the flip side of the reality is that American military technology generally performs extremely well in combat. Examples include Operation Desert Storm in 1991, the overthrow of the Taliban in Afghanistan in 2001, the rapid invasion of Iraq and Thunder Run through Baghdad in 2003, the dependable deployment and sustained support of U.S. forces in the field during all these and other operations, the magnificent intelligence and command and control networks that facilitate rapid targeting of extremists on the battlefield and around the world, and the development of drone technology to complement earlier breakthroughs in areas like stealth and precision munitions. These are testaments to scientific and industrial excellence on the part of America's laboratories, weapons development teams, and manufacturers.

In the 1990s, reducing procurement budgets was a prime way of slashing defense budgets after the cold war ended. Indeed, annual procurement budgets were reduced by two-thirds relative to earlier Reagan-era highs. But that was an unusual situation. The United States at that point could take a "procurement holiday" of sorts since it had recently bought so much new equipment during that Reagan buildup, and since the reduction of the combat force structure allowed older equipment to be selectively retired first. Today, there is no large inventory of new equipment that can allow us such a budgetary reprieve in the coming decade. In particular, much of that Reagan-era equipment is still around, but now in need of replacement—not just to modernize the force, but simply to keep it safe and reliable.

The defense industry faced major challenges during those 1990s cutbacks, of course. Softening the pain to an extent, however, was the fact that the 1980s had been a quite good decade for defense business. In addition, even though the economy was mediocre in the early part of the 1990s in the United States—and even though defense cutbacks exacerbated the difficulty in some cases[2]—the situation rapidly improved. As the 1990s progressed, the general condition of the U.S. economy strengthened, creating new jobs in other sectors.

Today, of course, the national economy is much weaker. The defense sector is also smaller. The number of workers in aerospace and defense is down from more than 1 million in 1991 to just over 600,000 two decades later, exemplifying the tendency of the U.S. manufacturing base to lose lots of jobs over that period.[3] After mergers and consolidations, there are now just five major contractors in the defense business—Boeing, Raytheon, Northrop Grumman, Lockheed Martin, and General Dynamics. Often only one or two contractors are capable of creating a given type of weapon system. As such, the health of the industrial base needs to be kept in mind, since budgets are not large enough to guarantee a diverse and strong national security industrial base absent considerable care and attentiveness.[4] Certain capabilities could simply be lost and would take years to recreate.[5] The ability to keep costs in check through competition could also be lost.[6]

The situation is complicated further by another trend. Even though current acquisition budgets are sizeable in real-dollar terms, the growing cost of weaponry means that these budgets typically fund fewer major programs than was the case in previous years. That reality is reinforced by the fact that more of today's acquisition budget is devoted to research and development rather than production—perhaps a reasonable approach at a time of rapid technology change, but still a tendency that squeezes procurement accounts.

When tackling defense modernization questions, several core realities need to be kept in mind. The first is that few, if any, of today's expensive systems can fairly be described as "cold war legacy weapons," in other words, weapons the Pentagon retains out of inertia but should have eliminated twenty years ago. No weapon today is being justified on the grounds that it might be needed against a Soviet-like threat. Rather, worries that adversaries could employ advanced surface-to-air, air-to-air, antiship, and ground attack missiles, quiet diesel submarines, sophisticated mines, and other such assets drive the Pentagon's desires for stealth, speed, maneuverability, survivability, and related characteristics in future weaponry.

Another central fact about defense modernization is that some state-of-the-art weapons will always cost more than originally foreseen. Cost growth is inevitable during the invention process. Typical increases are in the range of 25 to 50 percent, leaving aside the effects of changed plans, delays, and the like.[7] Another key dilemma: When the Pentagon chooses to build fewer of a given type of weapon, unit production costs usually go up by at least 10 percent and sometimes more because economies of scale are lost. This dynamic consumes some of the savings that might have been initially expected. Another sober reality concerns the cancellation of new weapons programs: Unless the combat units that were to receive the new weaponry are simply eliminated, cancelling a weapon would not change the need to buy *something* serviceable, safe, and reliable to equip those units. As a rule, weapons costing at least half as much as the canceled systems will be needed.[8] With today's Air Force tactical aircraft averaging more than twenty years in age, as well as Navy and Marine Corps aircraft averaging more than fifteen years, purchasing some types of new planes cannot be deferred.[9] The same thing goes for other areas of technology.

Savings are nonetheless possible. Consider again tactical combat aircraft. Even as drones have become much more effective, even as precision-guided ordnance has become devastatingly accurate, and even as real-time surveillance and information grids have evolved rapidly, plans for modernizing manned combat systems have remained essentially at previous levels.

All together, the Air Force, Navy, and Marine Corps still plan to buy nearly 2,500 F-35 combat jets at a total acquisition price of more than $300 billion in constant 2013 dollars. Production is just beginning at low rates, with the big ramp-up expected in the next few years. The Pentagon will spend about $15 billion annually on the plane starting in mid-decade. Three-fourths of the projected funds are yet to be spent. The Pentagon's independent cost assessment office believes the average unit procurement price could be 15 to 20 percent higher than official estimates, exceeding $115 million per plane in 2013 dollars. And once purchased, the same office estimates that the F-35 will also cost one-third more to operate in real terms than planes like the F-16 and F-18 that it is replacing.[10] Analysts like Chuck Spinney and Lane Pierrot predicted such problems for years.

It is important to acknowledge some strengths of the F-35, though, and to challenge some common criticisms. Some have opposed the Marine Corps variant of the plane (the F-35B), with its extra engine as needed for short or vertical takeoffs and landings. But in fact, that variant has value for an era in which airfields are increasingly vulnerable to precision ordnance. The United States needs enough F-35Bs to be able to populate bases nearest potential combat zones, such as the Gulf states (for scenarios involving Iran) and Okinawa (in regard to China). As Marine Corps commandant General James Amos has noted, there are ten times as many 3,000 foot runways in the world adequate for such short-takeoff jets as there are 8,000 foot runways suitable for conventional aircraft—and the Marines can lay down an expeditionary 3,000 foot runway in a matter of days in other places.[11]

An alternative concept for F-35 production could be as follows: Purchase a total of 1,250 instead of 2,500. Leave the Marine Corps plan largely as is, scaling back only by 10 to 20 percent to account more fully for the proven capacity of unmanned aerial vehicles to carry out some missions previously handled by manned aircraft. Cancel the Navy variant (the F-35C), with its relatively limited range compared with likely needs—buying more F/A-18 E/F Super Hornets in the meantime while committing more firmly to development of a longer-range unmanned carrier-capable attack aircraft.[12] The X-47B unmanned system, which completed demonstration tests on a carrier in 2012, is scheduled to conduct flight operations from an aircraft carrier in 2013, so this capability is progressing.[13] Reduce Air Force numbers, currently expected to exceed 1,700 F-35 planes, by almost half.

Of the 800 planes that the Air Force was counting on, but would not get under this approach, the difference can be made up in the following ways. First, cut back 200 planes by eliminating two tactical fighter wings. Second, view the 200 large combat-capable unmanned aerial vehicles (UAVs) currently owned by the Air Force, together with the 300 or more on the way, as viable replacements for some manned fighter planes. The Air Force is buying the equivalent of five wings of large UAVs; perhaps it could transform two manned combat wings into unmanned combat aircraft wings as a result.[14] For the remaining planes, employ further purchases of F-16 jets and refurbishments of existing F-16s to make up the difference as needed.[15]

This approach will produce net savings of some $60 billion in Air Force aircraft purchase costs. The F-16 option is still available since the production line is currently making aircraft for Morocco and Oman among others, but it may not remain open for more than a couple of years, so this option would have to be exercised fairly promptly to make economic sense.[16] Additional savings in the Marine Corps and Navy will add up to another $20 billion to $25 billion.

Average annual savings from this alternative approach to F-35 production might be $5 billion. Over time up to another $2 billion a year or so in savings would be achievable in operating accounts from the sum total of all these changes in tactical aircraft. These savings will not kick in right away, since it is important to get the F-35 production line working efficiently to keep unit costs in check. More of the savings will accrue in the 2020s.

It should also be remembered that a fair amount of risk is inherent in this alternative plan, since entirely canceling the F-35C Navy version of the plane will leave the Navy with less stealthy aircraft over the next decade. This is probably a tolerable risk but is not a trivial one.[17]

Following the logic of the discussion on aircraft, I would propose evaluating other existing weapons modernization plans with an eye toward streamlining or canceling several of them. Weapons making maximum use of the computer and communications revolutions should be considered highest priority. These arguably offer the greatest benefit for the most reasonable price tag—the best bang for the buck. Current trends in precision munitions, in computer technology, and in related fields such as robotics offer tremendous opportunities.[18] Weapons that appear redundant should be protected less.[19] Weapons that perform poorly—whether technically or financially—should of course be reassessed.[20]

In this light, changes to several areas of defense modernization beyond the F-35 example discussed above should be seriously considered.[21] To begin, even more dramatic change is possible in a program known as the Littoral Combat Ship (LCS), designed to replace the country's frigates and some mine warfare ships. It was supposed to be an efficient, economical vessel with innovative concepts. But it has gradually evolved into something more like a traditional frigate with a half-billion-dollar price tag per vessel and with questionable survivability, according to the Pentagon's director of operational test and evaluation.[22] Rather than build more than fifty, as planned, the Navy should adopt a new approach. The Navy should consider buying just ten to twenty such vessels (either LCS or the Coast Guard's National Security Cutter) to serve as "mother ships" for a new type of networked naval capability featuring other, cheaper vessels. Some could be low-draft, high-speed ships like the Stiletto, which captures its own wake and thereby travels fast and efficiently—along the lines of what the LCS was itself originally supposed to do. These other vessels could take advantage of new technology such as advanced mine countermeasure capabilities that can be deployed on numerous platforms besides the LCS.[23] Someday soon, more unmanned vessels also could contribute to operations in shallow waters. Resulting savings would be at least $1 billion a year in acquisition and additional amounts in reduced longer-term operating costs.

The Marine Corps can also reduce planned purchases of the V-22 Osprey. This tilt-rotor plane, which takes off and lands like a helicopter but flies like a propeller craft, is impressive, and many of the earlier

problems with its technology have been worked out. But the added survivability it provides in battle is modest, for the simple reason that, like
a helicopter, it will be exposed in the vertical parts of its flight. The
added cost is not worth it for routine missions, as reinforced by the
fact that the Army is not buying Ospreys. Viewing the V-22 as a niche
capability and instead buying existing-generation helicopters to replace
aging lift capabilities would produce annual savings of nearly $1 billion
for a number of years.

5

Nuclear Weapons, Missile Defense, and Intelligence

Substantial defense spending savings can be realized in the broad domain of strategic capabilities and intelligence functions. The sums are not as large as they used to be, in the former case, and not as easy to scrutinize as the rest of the Defense Department budget, in the latter case. But several billion dollars a year in possible savings are at stake.

Even though it has already come down dramatically since the end of the cold war, spending on nuclear weapons can be further reduced. The United States does not need all of the more than 1,500 strategic warheads allowed by the "New START" arms treaty with Russia, plus several thousand additional tactical and surplus warheads that are entirely unconstrained by this or any other international agreement. Ideally, a treaty could be struck between Washington and Moscow to reduce total warhead holdings—strategic, tactical, and surplus—on each side from 2,000 to 2,500.[1]

But even without such an accord, savings are possible and even desirable. The United States can scale back submarines and ICBMs. Remaining submarines could be loaded with their full complement of warheads, if that was considered truly necessary, to sustain numerical parity with Russia. For those who feel that any nuclear cuts must be at least partially reversible, moreover, the U.S. bomber fleet provides a hedge. Today most of it is focused on conventional military missions, but more aircraft could be returned to dual purposes.

This change in approach would still keep us at nuclear parity with Russia. And it would save money—in the submarine and missile forces of the Department of Defense, and in the nuclear-related activities of the Department of Energy. Termination of the "D5" submarine-launched, nuclear-tipped ballistic missile program would be possible. The current fleet of fourteen nuclear-armed submarines could be reduced to eight. This would still allow a robust submarine-based leg of the triad but with more warheads per missile and more per submarine. The submarine leg of the triad is exceedingly survivable, and as such more risk can be accepted in its overall size.

Moreover, when existing Trident submarines and D5 missiles require replacement, current technologies will likely be adequate, as they constitute highly survivable and reliable systems. There is no need for big research and development projects and no need for a better ballistic-missile submarine in the future. Current plans to start delivering a new class of submarine in the late 2020s and ultimately build a dozen at a total cost of up to $100 billion are unnecessary (though most of the savings will accrue after the next ten years). Even if Trident submarines prove nearly as expensive to produce as the new class would have been, savings largely in research and development accounts could range into the many billions of dollars.

There are also ways to save in the land-based force. Half of the land-based Minuteman ICBM missiles could be retired. More of the U.S. treaty allowance of weapons could instead be attributed to the bomber force, as noted. Thankfully, the Air Force is already considering whether the Minuteman ICBM, now expected to endure to between 2020 and 2030, can be refurbished to last even longer, until 2050; this policy should be pursued but for an ICBM force only half as large as today's of 450.[2]

The Department of Energy's nuclear weapons assets could be scaled back as well. One of the country's two main weapons laboratories, Lawrence Livermore in northern California, would gradually leave the nuclear weapons business for the most part, while keeping very active in other areas of modern science. No dedicated new facility to make the plutonium "pits" at the heart of most weapons would be needed either, since the existing small facility at Los Alamos could be used as the arsenal continued to shrink in the years ahead, and since the pits are holding up very well.[3] In the shorter term, the $10 billion effort to refurbish the B61 bomb could be scaled back by half or more in numbers of warheads and the changes to be made per warhead, focusing just on safety and reliability. That program seeks to modify a grand total of just over 300 warheads of several different variants—an inefficient way to sustain future arsenal reliability.[4] Annual savings from all the above would total about $2.5 billion.[5]

The United States can also further reduce spending on missile defense. Missile defense is important, and is hardly the anachronism of U.S.-Russian nuclear competition of the cold war era that critics sometimes imply. But it remains somewhat overfunded, with too many systems in various stages of development and deployment. Current programs include upgrades to the ground-based strategic systems in California and Alaska, Aegis sea-based theater defense, THAAD land-based theater defense, and two land-based short-range defense systems including the Patriot and also the MEADS program, the latter in partnership with European allies. Annual savings from canceling the Patriot or the MEADS could average close to $1 billion a year over the coming decade.[6]

What about spending on the intelligence community? The budget of the American intelligence community is about $80 billion a year at present. It is found within the 050 national defense budget—and principally within the budget of the Department of Defense.

There is no getting around the fact that U.S. spending for intelligence is quite large—bigger in fact than any other country's entire military budget with the exception of China's. It has also more than doubled over the last dozen years or so, to the extent that occasional public disclosures of its aggregate size allow such comparisons to be made. The CIA added 50 percent more operations officers and analysts after 9/11.[7] In the interest of secrecy, little additional information is commonly provided to understand how the budget breaks down among the intelligence community's 16 organizations—from the CIA to the National Security Agency to the National Geospatial Agency to the Defense Intelligence Agency, as well as the intelligence units of each military service and each unified command.[8]

The intelligence world has come under criticism in recent years, some of it deserved, for various failings. It did not synthesize and understand the warnings that a major attack was in the making prior to 9/11. Its incorrect view that Iraq had weapons of mass destruction and its on-again/off-again warnings about Iran's progress toward a possible nuclear weapons capability have complicated American foreign policy and caused major fallout. But it is also important to recall that intelligence is an inherently difficult and uncertain business because much of it concerns trying to read other people's minds and predict the future.[9]

In addition to its challenges in regard to terrorism, the intelligence community also has taken on new tasks in recent years, notably the huge growth in cybersecurity concerns. It also has to contend with the growing vulnerability of its satellites due to trends in technology.[10] And at a time of uncertainty in the international environment due to the rise of many new powers, its overall activities remain at least as important as ever.

Yet some of the expansion of intelligence capabilities may have gone too far. The Defense Intelligence Agency more than doubled in size over the last decade. A multitude of new organizations was created. And far more contractors were hired to support these efforts. Total increases in personnel may have been in the range of 100,000. The increases were understandable in response to an immediate and urgent threat, as al Qaeda and related groups posed at the time. But while the threat remains, there is now much more capacity to counter it, and the wastefulness typically associated with rapid buildups should now be addressed. So significant belt-tightening is indeed appropriate in the intelligence world.[11]

Before he left office in 2011, and before the intensity of deficit reduction efforts so dramatically picked up, Secretary of Defense Robert Gates had set a goal to reduce the Pentagon's contractor workforce by a total of 30 percent over three years—largely in intelligence-related fields. That goal, already factored into previous defense budget reduction efforts, makes sense—and may be an ambitious enough savings target for now. It is possible that the intelligence community is pursuing too many big ticket items like expensive satellites, but it is difficult to know that from the almost nonexistent public record.

Carrying out the Gates reforms, while saving at most a couple billion dollars more in annual satellite-related expenses from the broader intelligence community, would seem an ambitious goal that we will do well to achieve. Intelligence probably should not be cut by quite as great a proportion as other elements of national security spending. The resulting yearly budget can be reduced by $3 billion to $5 billion, though some of this is likely under way already.

6

MILITARY COMPENSATION AND PENTAGON REFORMS

Beyond cutting forces and weapons, are there ways to save money without directly reducing combat capability? Chuck Hagel, the new defense secretary, has called the Pentagon "bloated," and in some ways it surely is. But Pentagon comptroller Bob Hale has noted that eliminating actual waste in the Department of Defense (DoD) often is difficult in a classic economic sense; more often, when cuts are made, capabilities are lost, even if they are less important ones.[1] In other words, the reform process is important, feasible, and promising as a way to save money—but there is no free lunch and there are few painless cuts. In that spirit, I begin below with an area of obviously considerable political sensitivity: military compensation.

Military Compensation

The United States is a democracy at war asking young men and women who volunteer for the job to defend the country and its security. Few would deny that the United States has a special debt to its troops.

The country also has the best military in history—and that is not an American birthright, as we know from other periods in history, like the immediate post-Vietnam days of the so-called "hollow force." Rather, it is largely because of the unbelievable quality of men and women in uniform at present. The country must continue to make military service appealing enough that such individuals continue to join, and remain in, the force. A decade of war has, alas, produced some worrisome trends. This is evident not only in terms of the mental and physical health of those who have been at war, but in terms of somewhat weaker aptitude scores among typical Army recruits, since the Army has borne the brunt of the wars and as such has had some challenges in continuing to attract top-tier soldiers. The trend has not been particularly severe. For example, by one measure, the percentage of new enlistees scoring above the median on the Armed Forces Qualification Test has dipped only from 65 percent to 62 percent over the last decade. But the trend needs to be tracked carefully, and policymakers need to avoid such stark changes in compensation that they would risk the quality and morale of the all-volunteer force.[2]

And while making greater use of simulators and the like where possible, the country must also continue to train military personnel under realistic conditions to the high standards that have characterized the post-Vietnam American military for a generation.[3] Any discussion of reform needs to begin with these principles clearly in mind.

The American military is good largely because it is an adaptive, learning organization. It has a tradition, going back to Vietnam, of training realistically and then carrying out "after action reviews" in which everyone is expected to be self-critical. It does this in wartime extremely well, too. But this is only possible because resources are adequate to train realistically and because the military's educational and compensation systems are good enough to attract many of our best and brightest youth into national service.

Several principles are key in deciding on future military compensation policy. First, deployed troops and wounded warriors, as well as their families, must be helped at all costs; we are doing better and better in this task but still not well enough. Specifically, the budget of the Veterans Administration needs to be fenced off from the kinds of analyses conducted here, as it provides care for injured and disabled veterans and their families, and any reforms therein must be done very carefully. Indeed, some augmentations in veterans' services are warranted, such as greater ability for individuals suffering from mental challenges to seek help in the private sector at government expense, as an added option to what currently exists (as suggested by retired General Jack Keane and others).

Second, the country needs to provide incentives for young, technically skilled, and highly motivated people to join and stay in the military. Third, while the nation cannot realistically make military service a lucrative career path per se, it needs to be sure to provide reasonable compensation for volunteers risking their lives for their nation.

Fortunately, military pay compares favorably with the private sector in the United States today. Private-sector wages, especially for middle-class and blue-collar jobs, have stagnated in recent decades while military compensation has continued to improve. On average, for individuals of a given age and educational background, the American armed forces actually pay substantially *better* today than does the private sector. Averaged across enlisted personnel, total military compensation is about $50,000 a year, more than $20,000 greater than for jobs with similar educational requirements and age and experience levels in the civilian economy. That is in large part because military jobs carry benefits above and beyond wages—such as health care and retirement—that can further favor those in uniform. Put differently, averaged across the military, and counting all benefits, enlisted military personnel make more than 90 percent of all civilians in the country for individuals of the same age, experience, and educational qualifications. This situation is generally similar for officers.[4]

Military compensation per active-duty service member, according to a 2012 Congressional Budget Office (CBO) study, increased to roughly $100,000 in 2012 from $70,000 in 2000.[5] (These costs do not include the dramatically higher expenditures for Veterans Administration benefits that one would expect, and that the country should fully support, after a decade at war.)

But that CBO figure is an average. Some problems exist. Technical experts in areas like computers may still make less in the military than they would in the private sector. Those who do twenty-year careers in the military get generous retirement packages, and those doing less get nothing. Middle-aged retirees who go on to other jobs, with those generous retirement packages, also get deals on health care that the rest of the country can only dream about in this day and age. Many of these things can and should change. The United States can actually make military compensation more fair and also moderately less expensive.

To begin, the Department of Defense should increase military compensation more selectively in the future. General pay increases could be held to the rate of inflation, with bonuses of various types used to address specific shortfalls in the force structure. The CBO puts annual savings at about $1.5 billion.[6] One could make a case for an actual pay freeze for two to three years, in fact, with no inflation adjustment at all over that period of time. That could save at least another $5 billion a year, indefinitely into the future. But in light of the other reforms I advocate below, my preference would be not to turn to this pay-freeze option now.

One reform idea is to eliminate stateside military exchanges and especially commissaries. These kinds of on-base stores are popular with military families, but in the era of Wal-Mart, Cosco, Home Depot, and Best Buy they are less important than before and are no longer a prudent use of taxpayers' money. At least $1.5 billion a year can be saved in this way.[7] (As a compromise, some could be retained in those few locations without large outlets.)

Even bigger savings can be found by increasing cost-sharing within the military health care program. The TRICARE system provides an extremely good deal to military families. While this is understandable to a degree, it has arguably gone too far, not only exceeding the generosity of plans in the civilian economy but encouraging excessive use of health care (due to the low costs).

One issue is that TRICARE is available to retirees and their families. Some retirees argue that they were promised free health care for life when joining the military. Well, if they were, it was in many cases a type of health care radically different—and radically cheaper, perhaps by 75 percent or more depending on their age—than what is available today. No one would begrudge wounded warriors the best of care; the issue here, rather, is the cost-sharing system of copayments and enrollment fees for the typical military family, including retiree families. Reforms that retained a generous military health care system but with cost-sharing at a level more similar to that in the civilian economy could save $6 billion a year.[8]

And finally, it is simply time to change the military retirement system, going back to ideas temporarily implemented under Ronald Reagan in the 1980s. The military retirement system is arguably too generous at twenty years of service and not generous enough for those leaving the armed forces sooner. Indeed, those leaving the military after one or two or three tours of duty get nothing—an unfairness to many of our combat veterans, among others. The generous benefits for those staying within DoD for twenty years continue despite the fact that second careers after the military have become much more common, and military pay relative to private sector pay has greatly improved. Providing a modest benefit, analogous to a 401K in the private sector, or eligibility for military personnel to participate in the Thrift Savings Plan as it exists for civilian government employees (which involves matching government funds for those willing to save for retirement), would improve fairness. Higher amounts could be contributed by the government for those who have served in dangerous zones.

This new retirement system would also save money. The Hadley/Perry independent panel that assessed the Pentagon's 2010 Quadrennial Defense Review made this general argument.[9] A recent Defense Business Board study suggests savings that could approach $10 billion a year over the next twenty years. Even if a modified version of the plan only half as ambitious were instituted, and savings accumulated gradually, it is likely that $2 billion to $3 billion a year could be saved over the next decade.[10]

Reforms and Efficiencies

When trying to cut the budget, it is essential to search for waste, fraud, and abuse. It is also good politics. Alas, this is challenging.[11] The reason is not just that entrenched interests often oppose reform. It is also that the prospect of real cost savings is often uncertain or even illusory, and that up-front expenses are needed to implement reforms (meaning that short-term savings can actually be negative).

A case in point is base closures. The first four rounds were a relative success—more expensive to implement than initially foreseen (with a combined up-front implementation cost of $25 billion), and slower to yield savings, but still a net benefit to the Department of Defense and the taxpayer. However, the 2005 round, originally expected to yield a net savings of $35 billion over twenty years, is now expected to yield just $10 billion, with most of those savings toward the end of the process. Initial implementation costs, originally projected at $21 billion, wound up closer to $35 billion.[12] Some of these unfavorable revisions to original estimates may have been due to the fact that a fifth round of base closures had fewer obvious targets for major savings than the first four; some of them frankly could have been due to questionable analysis, planning, and implementation.

Given that history, the Department of Defense's recent requests for additional base closure rounds were frowned upon by Congress. However, they probably do remain a good idea. The 2005 round was unusual, with its focus on increasing joint operations rather than efficiency, suggesting that future rounds could do better. They will likely yield eventual savings of $2 billion to $3 billion a year, comparable to the first four rounds.[13] That said, net savings over a decade would be very modest as those types of savings tend not to be realized for a half decade, and in the early years implementation costs can be significant.

If one or two rounds of subsequent base closures save a net of $10 billion over the next ten years, we will be doing well.[14]

Savings from some possible reforms are even harder to gauge in advance than those for base closures. A number of reforms are being attempted, including the Better Buying Power Initiative of Frank Kendall, under secretary of defense for Acquisition, Technology, and Logistics, which emphasizes development of a career-oriented professional acquisition workforce, among other goals.[15] But knowing what will be saved is quite difficult. For example, in 2012 the Government Accountability Office (GAO) released two studies on two different defense reform concepts that underscored the uncertainties involved in predicting savings. One study considered whether the Department of Defense could use "strategic sourcing" more frequently to buy supplies in bulk and at discount across the department. But of course, many Pentagon purchases are of a much different nature than those of private corporations. As such, the GAO had difficulty predicting savings. At one point in its report, for admittedly illustrative purposes, it spoke of savings of up to $50 billion a year (for DoD and several other agencies combined) from this possible reform. At another point, once getting more specific and analytical, its estimate was closer to $5 billion or less (for just DoD in that case), and even that figure was highly notional. Moreover, that would be a medium-term goal, not an immediately attainable objective. This is not to criticize GAO, but to note the great imprecision involved in making such predictions.[16] There is also a case for streamlining reporting requirements for acquisition projects—which could save money in terms of reducing the DoD workforce doing the reporting, but at a somewhat higher risk of cost overruns or abuses by contractors.[17] It makes sense to reexamine reporting requirements, but it is difficult to predict a specific savings figure associated with such an effort.

As another example, GAO wrote about the possible advantages to entering into long-term contracts with private contractors for maintaining weapons and other hardware. But GAO also noted that it had cost nearly $20 billion in facilities and other investments to implement such contracts for a group of ten weapons systems. Any net savings in areas such as reform and further privatization of maintenance work would therefore take considerable time to be realized.[18]

There is no reason to oppose possible reforms just because of such uncertainties. But since DoD is already counting on $60 billion in ten-year savings from reforms and efficiencies in its current budget plan, there should be considerable wariness about assuming even more savings from additional measures. Savings in areas that have been untapped to date may range into the low billions of dollars a year—but only once implemented, over time.[19] All that said, it is still necessary to make the effort, and keep at it.[20]

One useful idea is to close some additional commands and a war college, too. Secretary Robert Gates closed Joint Forces Command with possible annual savings in the low hundreds of millions of dollars. The process needs to continue further. Each military service has several major commands within its own institution. The individual services do not need all the component commands they have in geographic theaters—the Army in Korea, the Navy in Europe, for example—when many of these theaters have seen substantial U.S. military downsizing and when unified joint commands are also present.[21] Even for those headquarters that are retained, efficiencies are possible, as Mackenzie Eaglen of the American Enterprise Institute has argued recently. Many high-level military headquarters, within the Pentagon and outside of it, have grown in recent decades. The military makes use of larger staffs than most organizations, and it is not unreasonable to impose a uniform cut—perhaps 30 percent, in line with what Secretary Gates instituted for civilians supporting the intelligence community—in major DoD offices. Savings of at least several thousand personnel might follow, with annual savings of at least $500 million once carried out.[22]

Each service has at least one war college in an era when "jointness" is supposed to be the watchword, and when each service is at least one-third smaller than a quarter-century ago. With a smaller military, at least one of the war colleges—in Alabama, Virginia, Pennsylvania, and Rhode Island for the Air Force, Marine Corps, Army, and Navy, respectively—can be closed and its activities merged with the remaining colleges. Closing one would be roughly proportionate to the overall reductions in the size of the armed forces over the last twenty years. Indeed, there is a case to eliminate entirely the service-specific war colleges, retaining some but not all of the existing facilities for new joint institutions. More specialized institutions such as the Naval Postgraduate School should also be rethought. Corresponding changes might save up to $1 billion annually.

As noted, another round of base closures also makes sense. Since it is possible that future global developments may require at least a temporary increase in the size of the force at some future date, not all the closed facilities should be sold; the government should hold onto some extra land where it can add more basing on short notice if need be. But the annual costs of operating excess buildings and other facilities cannot be sustained and must be cut. Changes also might be considered abroad, in places such as Germany where, despite downsizing in recent decades, a large number of facilities remains. The overall U.S. troop presence in Europe probably should not be cut further, but existing forces can be consolidated. A round comparable in magnitude to previous efforts would, once changes are complete, save some $2 billion a year.

Another base-related matter concerns U.S. forces in the Western Pacific. Most established overseas bases for the United States are not excessively expensive, because the costs of personnel and equipment are virtually identical to what they would be for stateside forces and because allies often contribute to local costs for land and utilities and the like.[23] But the budgetary costs of current plans to relocate forces in Korea and Japan could range up to $50 billion over a number of years. Most of the cost would be associated with moving some 7,000 Marines from Okinawa, Japan, to Guam—costs that likely would be borne in large measure by Tokyo, if it can sort out the Japanese domestic politics and get the basic concept approved in the first place. Opposition on Okinawa to one aspect of the plan that would entail building a new air-field on a different part of the island may sink the whole concept.[24]

There are better ways to handle this situation with the Marine Corps and Okinawa. As Mike Mochizuki and I have argued, half the Marines could be brought to California instead of Guam, taking up space in barracks being evacuated by the downsizing of the Marine Corps. Japan could then be asked to help purchase enough maritime prepositioning ships and associated equipment for that same number of Marines, and to allow the military to homeport the ships in the main islands of Japan. In a future crisis, the ships could be sailed to where they were needed, and the California-based Marines could fly there to marry up with their weaponry. A modest-sized heliport rather than a full-fledged new airport could then be built on Okinawa to replace the Futenma Air Station's still-needed functions. Japan also could add a runway at its main Naha Airport on Okinawa that could be used commercially in peacetime but remain available for military operations in crisis or war. These changes in total would likely save the United States some half billion dollars a year over the next decade.

There are also more mundane efficiencies to be pursued. As one example, the Pentagon should revamp military traditions and perquisites such as business jets for many top flag officers. Yes, commanders in the field need their own mobility, but officers running domestic commands do not. An anecdote from the recent past illustrates the situation. Both the deputy secretary of state and deputy secretary of defense attended a conference in Colorado. The former flew out, commercial class, by himself. The latter arrived in a military jet with entourage—which was the jet's second trip to the site in as many weeks, since the week before an advance team had come to scout out the place. It is indeed important to protect our key public servants, but the excesses of the deputy defense secretary's trip were remarkable for a man not in the wartime chain of command and not an iconic or famous public figure. There are dozens of such planes that are superfluous, meaning that at least $200 million a year can be saved by eliminating them.

It is also time, with respect and admiration for their service, to scale back military bands. Yes, military morale is important and bands help. But today's deployed military has, in most cases, TV, hot food, and air conditioning; this is not to say that life is easy abroad, only that the nature of amenities and morale boosters has changed. And where troops in the field do not have such things because of their remote locations or dangerous circumstances, bands will have a hard time venturing in any case. Roughly $200 million a year can be saved in this way.

A final example of possible savings, championed by Senator Tom Coburn, is to close military schools in places where public schools—generally more cost-efficient—are available. Nearly 20,000 students could be involved: not huge numbers, but not budgetarily insignificant either. Several hundred million dollars in annual savings could eventually become possible.[25]

Through the combined effects of all of the above, more than $15 billion a year can be saved eventually—perhaps an amount approaching $20 billion. Some of these savings, but only a modest fraction, are assumed within DoD's plans as of early 2012. Realistically, given the time needed to phase in such changes, it will be an accomplishment to achieve close to $100 billion in ten-year savings, and much of that could be required simply to attain the $60 billion goal in efficiencies that the Pentagon has already counted on and assumed. But the available amounts of savings are quite substantial nonetheless.

7

CONCLUSION — AND THE IMPLICATIONS OF PROLONGED SEQUESTRATION OR THE EQUIVALENT

Defense spending cuts make sense only as part of a broader national effort of deficit reduction and economic renewal. The suggestions here are motivated not by any anti-defense agenda but rather by the goal of minimizing aggregate national security risk. There is no logic to doing so if entitlement policy, tax policy, and most other federal programs remain unchecked while the Pentagon is offered up as sacrificial lamb (along with domestic "discretionary" programs) in an unbalanced deficit reduction effort. However, done as part of a general national agenda of shared sacrifice, cuts of significant magnitude in defense may be feasible without requiring strategic retrenchment—and may be good for long-term national security.

Up to another $200 billion in aggregate ten-year military spending cuts in weapons, units, and other Pentagon expenses are reasonable. These cuts go beyond those already expected as part of a gradual reduction in the nation's costs for waging war abroad. The additional cuts may not translate into quite that much in actual reductions in the defense topline budget, however, because current plans (as of 2012) are optimistic—

they may cost more than expected. As such, some additional cuts in forces and weapons may be needed simply to comply with budgetary savings envisioned in the first tranche of the 2011 Budget Control Act (that is, the cuts sometimes reported as $487 billion over ten years, though more accurately understood as $350 billion relative to a Congressional Budget Office constant-dollar baseline). So the ideas here would be some $300 billion or so lesss severe than the cuts assumed under sequestration or a plan like the Simpson-Bowles 2010 effort.

Larger defense cuts that could approach another half trillion dollars over ten years, as under sequestration or the Simpson-Bowles deficit reduction plan, would be unwise. Yes, America's armed forces today are expensive, but that is for a good reason—they are a stabilizing element in the current global environment. Most other countries welcome American military power and choose to ally with it formally or informally, even as they sometimes complain about U.S. foreign policy. And if the military is expensive, that is also because you get what you pay for. While America's armed forces are costly on a per-person basis—which is the right thing to do, since a democracy with an all-volunteer force owes it to men and women in uniform to take good care of them—they are not particularly large in size.

With reductions of up to $200 billion relative to 2012 plans, the nation can avoid salary cuts for its troops or any hint of weakening resolve toward East Asia or the Persian Gulf. It can modernize forces enough that the most promising new technologies can be pursued in numbers adequate to equip those forces most likely to fight in key regions. It can retain ground forces large enough, even after the Afghanistan campaign winds down, to carry out another war if necessary (heaven forbid) without having to let down its guard elsewhere and steal forces from all other theaters to conduct the combat operation.

If instead the United States pursued another half trillion dollars in ten-year defense budget cuts, as under sequestration or the Simpson-Bowles plan, making for a cumulative total of nearly $1 trillion dollars or 15 to 20 percent, since 2011, these would require more dramatic changes in America's basic strategic approach to the world and to how it maintains the world's finest armed services. Such ideas are not unthinkable. They would not emasculate the country or deprive it of superpower status or immediately open the door to adventurism by aggressors abroad. I simply view them as excessive and ill-advised in light of the likely risks versus the expected benefits.

If such deep cuts happened anyway, three of the least debilitating ways to carry them out might be as follows.

First, rather than simply streamlining the active-duty Army and Marine Corps to sizes slightly below Clinton-era levels, these services might be cut by 25 percent, going much further than the Obama administration now plans. This would likely deprive the nation of the prompt capacity to conduct anything more than one large ground operation at a time, or perhaps one large operation plus a very modest additional one, even though recent history has demonstrated that multiple simultaneous missions are more than possible.

To make the math work, the Army might wind up with 400,000 active-duty soldiers under this approach, in contrast to more than half a million now and to some 475,000 in the Clinton and early Bush years. The Marine Corps might level off at 150,000 active-duty personnel. The combined total would be enough for one major operation, for example the unlikely but not unthinkable contingency of another war in Korea. It would also likely keep the Army large enough to retain its prestige as the world's best ground combat force and to facilitate foreign engagement globally in peacetime. But it would not allow enough capability for that role plus, at the same time, an ongoing mission similar to the one in Afghanistan today—or a substantial role in a future Syria operation, for example. It would effectively move ground force planning away from the two-war standard that has, however imperfectly and inexactly, undergirded American military strategy for decades. My fear is that such a cut would weaken deterrence. Since small- to mid-sized missions are the most likely ones in the future, it would be regrettable that America's capacity for quick response to a major regional war would be effectively called into doubt any time such operations were undertaken. Still, this approach could save $100 billion over a decade.

The second major change to achieve deep cuts could be in military compensation. Now more than $25,000 per person greater than at the start of the Bush administration, military compensation might be gradually returned toward 2001 levels. In chapter 6, I proposed some $10 billion in annual savings concerning health care and pension reform, among other things. In theory, even deeper cuts in military compensation could save another $15 billion, or up to $25 billion annually. That would, however, likely go too far. While econometrically imaginable, in light of all the increases in compensation in recent years, it would also risk sending a very negative message to men and women in uniform and would imperil the ability of the military to recruit and retain the best and brightest. It would amount to a multi-front cut to military compensation, across all major areas of current benefits, and could certainly jeopardize the integrity and quality of the all-volunteer force.

A third cut of comparable budgetary significance could be accomplished by cancelling the F-35 joint strike fighter outright coupled with a decision to buy more F-15, F-16, and F-18 vintage aircraft as well as unmanned aerial vehicles instead. This would deprive the country of a stealthy main attack jet and place America's hopes for an enduring technological edge in its small B-2 and F-22 aircraft fleets, together with improved precision-strike munitions and also future types of unmanned aircraft. Such a retrenchment would also amount to an invitation to China to close the technological gap with America much more quickly than might be possible otherwise. As such it does not make sense to me, even if it would be feasible in principle..

In the end, while the cuts required under sequestration or similar plans are unwise, the United States can and should attempt to find more modest savings in the defense budget. It should do so, however, only in the context of reestablishing national sacrifice and fiscal discipline across the government. America's defense spending levels are not inherently dangerous and are not grossly wasteful, even if the pre-sequestration plans that have undergirded administration defense policy through 2012 are somewhat greater and more expensive than they need to be. Sequestration goes too far, and does so too indiscriminately as well. But there is room to cut defense spending more modestly and prudently.

Appendix

Figure A-1. *U.S. National Defense Spending as a Percentage of Gross Domestic Product*

Percent

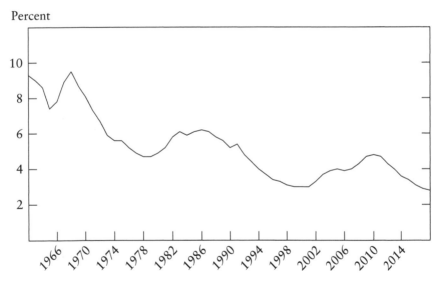

Source: Office of Management and Budget, *Historical Tables: Budget of the U.S. Government, Fiscal Year 2014* (Washington, April 2013), pp. 155–56.

Note: Figures are based on the president's budget request for 2014. Totals include all war and enacted supplemental funding and include Department of Energy national security spending.

Figure A-2. *U.S. National Defense Annual Outlays, Fiscal Years 1962–2018*

Billions of 2013 dollars

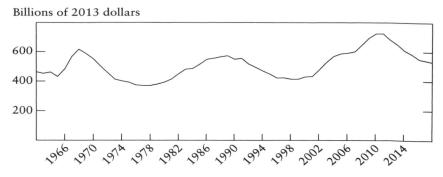

Source: Office of Management and Budget, *Historical Tables: Budget of the U.S. Government, Fiscal Year 2014* (Washington, April 2013), pp. 151–52.

Note: Figures are based on the president's budget request for 2014. Totals include all war and enacted supplemental funding and include Department of Energy national security spending.

Figure A-3. *Department of Defense Annual Budget Authority for Procurement and Research Development Test & Evaluation (RDT&E), Fiscal Years 1948–2014*

Billions of 2013 dollars

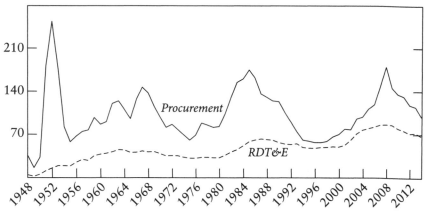

Source: Office of Management and Budget, *Historical Tables: Budget of the U.S. Government, Fiscal Year 2014* (Washington, April 2013), pp. 104–07. U.S. Department of Defense, National Defense Budget Estimates for FY 2012 (Washington, March 2011), pp. 123–28.

Note: Figures are based on the president's budget request for 2014. Totals include all enacted war and supplemental funding.

Table A-1. *Department of Defense Discretionary Budget Authority, by Title*

Billions of 2013 dollars

Category	2010	2011	2012	2013	2014
Military personnel	157.9	158.4	158.4	160.8	144.0
Operations and maintenance	293.6	305.2	286.8	263.3	210.2
Procurement	135.8	131.9	118.3	115.1	99.3
Research, development, testing, and evaluation	80.2	76.7	72.0	73.0	67.5
Military construction	22.6	16.0	11.4	11.4	9.5
Family housing	2.3	1.8	1.7	1.7	1.5
Revolving and management funds/other	4.0	1.4	6.9	4.9	89.4
Total	696.4	691.4	655.5	630.2	621.4

Source: Office of Management and Budget, *Historical Tables: Budget of the U.S. Government, Fiscal Year 2014* (Washington, April 2013), pp. 104–07.

Note: Figures are based on the president's budget request for 2014. Totals include all war and enacted supplemental funding. All figures are rounded.

Table A-2. *Cost Summary of Selected Weapons Systems, Selected Years*
Dollars in millions (as of December 31, 2011)

Weapons system	Base year	Base year dollars	Current dollars	Quantity
Army				
AB3A REMANUFACTURE	2010	10,468.7	11,896.6	639
AB3B NEW BUILD	2010	2,307.0	2,510.4	56
CH-47F	2005	10,614.8	12,147.4	512
EXCALIBUR	2007	1,654.6	1,679.0	7,474
FMTV	1996	11,594.2	18,921.3	85,488
GMLRS/GMLRS AW	2003	9,780.2	11,848.9	140,239
HIMARS	2003	3,711.6	4,388.4	894
IAMD	2009	4,856.6	5,791.6	296
JLENS	2005	5,850.0	7,151.0	16
LUH	2006	1,638.3	1,883.0	322
MQ-1C UAS GRAY EAGLE	2010	5,252.0	5,549.0	31
PATRIOT PAC-3	2002	9,084.0	9,205.8	1,159
PATRIOT/MEADS CAP—FIRE UNIT	2004	16,530.5	21,839.4	48
PATRIOT/MEADS CAP—MISSILE	2004	6,220.9	8,056.0	1,528
STRYKER	2004	8,276.9	8,534.7	2,096
UH-60M BLACK HAWK	2005	16,801.7	20,847.1	1,235
WIN-T INCREMENT 1	2007	3,798.0	3,879.7	1,677
WIN-T INCREMENT 2	2010	4,686.0	4,996.9	2,216
WIN-T INCREMENT 3	2009	15,807.9	18,813.2	3,428
Subtotal, Army		148,933.9	179,939.4	
Navy				
AGM-88E AARGM	2003	1,528.5	1,861.4	1,919
AIM-9X	1997	2,464.0	3,232.9	10,049
CEC	2002	4,123.3	4,310.7	272
CH-53K	2006	14,980.9	18,766.3	156
COBRA JUDY REPLACEMENT	2003	1,365.0	1,464.0	1
CVN 78 CLASS	2000	28,701.2	36,082.1	3
DDG 1000	2005	31,547.9	36,296.3	10
DDG 51	1987	16,953.7	20,117.5	23
E-2D AHE	2009	17,468.6	19,031.4	75
EA-18G	2004	7,530.8	8,636.4	84
F/A-18E/F	2000	38,884.7	41,637.3	458
H-1 UPGRADES (4BW/4BN)	2008	11,203.4	12,186.8	353
IDECM—IDECM Blocks 2/3	2008	1,410.9	1,535.2	12,809
IDECM—IDECM Block 4	2008	660.7	746.1	160
JHSV	2008	3,460.0	3,892.3	18
JPALS	2008	963.2	1,031.9	37

Table A-2. *Cost Summary of Selected Weapons Systems, Selected Years (Continued)*

Dollars in millions (as of December 31, 2011)

Weapons system	Base year	Base year dollars	Current dollars	Quantity
JSOW (BASELINE/UNITARY) —BASELINE/BLU-108	1990	3,566.3	4,898.7	16,124
JSOW (BASELINE/UNITARY) —UNITARY	1990	1,977.8	2,974.8	7,000
KC-130J	2010	9,233.9	9,881.8	104
LCS	2010	32,011.0	37,438.8	55
LHA 6 AMERICA CLASS	2006	2,877.4	3,093.5	1
LPD 17	1996	9,018.1	10,761.8	12
MH-60R	2006	10,627.0	11,424.7	254
MH-60S	1998	5,270.1	6,093.8	237
MQ-4C UAS BAMS	2008	12,224.5	15,172.3	70
MUOS	2004	5,768.9	6,810.6	6
NMT	2002	1,517.9	1,853.0	204
P-8A	2010	32,345.9	34,500.7	122
RMS	2006	1,279.6	1,449.4	54
SM-6	2004	5,281.1	6,597.2	1,200
SSN 774	1995	64,353.6	93,207.3	30
TACTICAL TOMAHAWK	1999	2,977.3	3,290.3	2,790
TRIDENT II MISSILE	1983	26,556.3	35,518.5	845
V-22	2005	50,250.4	53,253.4	458
VTUAV	2006	2,366.4	2,787.1	177
Subtotal, Navy		462,750.3	551,836.3	
Air Force				
AEHF	2002	5,800.7	6,085.7	3
AMRAAM	1992	12,278.2	13,112.4	15,450
B-2 EHF SATCOM AND COMPUTER INCREMENT 1	2007	659.7	706.1	21
C-130 AMP	2010	5,930.2	6,300.3	221
C-130J	1996	730.7	839.7	11
C-5 RERP	2008	7,146.6	7,694.1	52
FAB-T	2002	2,642.3	3,167.4	216
GBS	1997	451.4	497.1	346
GPS IIIA	2010	4,142.9	4,269.8	8
HC/MC-130 RECAPITALIZATION	2009	8,078.1	8,745.3	74
JASSM Baseline	2010	2,890.5	2,679.7	2,940
JASSM—ER	2010	2,195.0	2,301.4	2,507

(continued)

Table A-2. *Cost Summary of Selected Weapons Systems, Selected Years (Continued)*

Dollars in millions (as of December 31, 2011)

Weapons system	Base year	Base year dollars	Current dollars	Quantity
JDAM	1995	2,300.3	2,606.7	89,065
JPATS	2002	4,529.0	5,041.1	783
KC-46A	2011	43,518.2	51,700.2	179
MP-RTIP	2000	1,449.3	1,568.4	—
MQ-9 UAS REAPER	2008	10,751.3	11,834.8	391
NAS	2005	1,373.2	1,421.1	93
NAVSTAR GPS—SPACE & CONTROL	2000	5,015.6	5,120.9	33
NAVSTAR GPS—USER EQUIPMENT	2000	797.8	874.4	—
NPOESS	2002	5,538.0	6,117.6	6
RQ-4A/B UAS GLOBAL HAWK	2000	4,350.3	5,394.0	63
SBIRS HIGH	1995	3,679.5	4,147.3	5
SDB II	2010	4,577.5	5,210.4	17,163
WGS	2010	3,610.6	3,539.7	7
Subtotal, Air Force		144,436.9	160,975.6	
DoD				
AMF JTRS	2008	7,758.6	9,034.3	27,102
BMDS	2002	75,534.0	86,998.0	—
CHEM DEMIL—ACWA	2011	2,596.3	2,430.4	—
CHEM DEMIL—CMA	1994	11,513.7	12,879.9	29,060
F-35 AIRCRAFT	2012	178,478.7	194,351.7	2,866
F-35 ENGINE	2012	35,229.5	38,648.3	2,852
JTRS GMR	2002	14,437.2	19,112.9	108,388
JTRS HMS	2011	9,889.2	10,717.0	328,674
JTRS NED	2002	812.9	914.4	—
MIDS	2003	1,824.8	1,818.9	2,964
Subtotal, DoD		338,074.9	376,905.8	

Source: U.S. Department of Defense, Selected Acquisition Report (SAR) Summary Tables, March 2012 (as of December 31, 2011) (www.acq.osd.mil/ara/am/sar/SST-2011-12.pdf).

Note: Totals may not add up because of rounding. Each weapon system is assigned a base year based on key milestones in its development; costs as expressed in base year dollars are measured in that base year's constant dollars. All procurement as well as research, development, test, and evaluation are included. Actual costs can grow even more.

Notes

Chapter 1

1. See Heather L. Messera, Brendan Orino, and Peter W. Singer, "D.C.'s New Guard: What Does the Next Generation of American Leaders Think?" Brookings Institution, 2011 (www.brookings.edu/~/media/research/files/reports/2011/2/young%20leaders%20singer/02_young_leaders_singer.pdf).

2. See, for example, John Keegan, *The First World War* (New York: Alfred A. Knopf, 1999), pp. 10–18.

3. On climate change, for example, see Kurt M. Campbell and others, *The Age of Consequences: The Foreign Policy and National Security Implications of Global Climate Change* (Washington: Center for a New American Security, November 1, 2007) (www.cnas.org/files/documents/publications/CSIS-CNAS_AgeofConsequences_November07.pdf); for a very good paper on the biological weapons risk, see Richard Danzig, *Preparing for Catastrophic Bioterrorism: Toward a Long-Term Strategy for Limiting the Risk* (Washington: Center for Technology and National Security Policy, 2008).

4. See International Crisis Group, *Stirring Up the South China Sea*, Asia Report 223 (Washington: April 2012); Michael Wines, "China's Rising Military Officers Harbor Deep Suspicion of U.S.," *International Herald Tribune*, October 8, 2010, p. 1; and John

Pomfret, "U.S. Takes Tougher Stance with China," *Washington Post,* July 30, 2010, p. 1.

5. On this point, see Stephen G. Brooks, G. John Ikenberry, and William C. Wohlforth, "Lean Forward: In Defense of American Engagement," *Foreign Affairs,* vol. 92, no. 1 (January/February 2013), pp. 130–42; for an alternative view see Barry R. Posen, "The Case for a Less Activist Foreign Policy," *Foreign Affairs,* vol. 92, no. 1 (January/February 2013), pp. 116–29.

6. Congressional Budget Office, *Long-Term Implications of the 2012 Future Years Defense Program* (Washington: Congressional Budget Office, 2011), p. vii (www.cbo.gov/ftpdocs/122xx/doc12264/06-30-11_FYDP.pdf).

7. Office of Management and Budget, *Historical Tables, Fiscal Year 2012* (Government Printing Office, 2011), pp. 145–47.

8. See, for example, Secretary of State Hillary Rodham Clinton, "Remarks on United States Foreign Policy," Council on Foreign Relations, Washington, D.C., September 8, 2010 (www.state.gov/secretary/rm/2010/09/146917.htm); speech by Secretary of Defense Robert Gates at the Eisenhower Library, Abilene, Kansas, May 8, 2010 (www.defense.gov/speeches/speech.aspx?speechid=1467); and remarks by Admiral Mike Mullen at the Detroit Economic Club Luncheon, August 26, 2010 (www.jcs.mil/speech.aspx?ID=1445).

9. "Admiral Mike Mullen: 'National Debt Is Our Biggest Security Threat,'" *Huffington Post,* June 24, 2010 (www.huffingtonpost.com/2010/06/24/adm-mike-mullen-national_n_624096.html).

10. Richard Haass of the Council on Foreign Relations coined this phrase; see, for example, Richard N. Haass, *War of Necessity, War of Choice* (New York: Simon and Schuster, 2009).

11. Office of Management and Budget, *Historical Tables: Budget of the U.S. Government, Fiscal Year 2011* (Government Printing Office, 2010), p. 146.

12. International Institute for Strategic Studies, *The Military Balance 2010* (Oxfordshire, England: Routledge, 2010), p. 468.

13. Office of Management and Budget, *Historical Tables,* pp. 62, 83, and Office of Management and Budget, *Historical Tables, Fiscal Year 2013* (Government Printing Office, 2012), pp. 147–49.

14. Office of Management and Budget, *Fiscal Year 2013 Budget of the U.S. Government,* pp. 240–46.

15. For two analysts advocating stronger possible responses, see Ariel Cohen and Robert E. Hamilton, *The Russian Military and the Georgia War: Lessons and Implications* (Carlisle, Pa.: Strategic Studies Institute, 2011), p. vii.

16. U.S. Energy Information Administration, "International Energy Outlook 2010," Department of Energy, Washington, July 2010, pp. 30–37 (www.eia.doe.gov/oiaf/ieo).

Chapter 2

1. Office of the Under Secretary of Defense (Comptroller), *National Defense Budget Estimates for 2012* (Washington: Department of Defense, 2011), p. 232 (http://comptroller.defense.gov/defbudget/fy2012/FY12_Green_Book.pdf).

2. Secretary of Defense Robert Gates, *Quadrennial Defense Review Report* (Washington: Department of Defense, February 2010), p. 46.

3. For discussions of the force-sizing debates in this period, see, for example, Frederick W. Kagan, *Finding the Target: The Transformation of American Military Policy* (New York: Encounter Books, 2006), pp. 196–97 and 281–86; and 2d ed.(Brookings, 2002), pp. 9–17 and 63–71.

4. Robert Gates, *Quadrennial Defense Review Report*, p. vi.

5. Secretary of Defense Leon Panetta, "Sustaining U.S. Global Leadership: Priorities for 21st Century Defense," January 2012 (www.defense.gov/news/defense_strategic_guidance.pdf).

6. Robert P. Haffa Jr., *Rational Methods, Prudent Choices: Planning U.S. Forces* (Washington: National Defense University, 1988), pp. 77–82 and 110–26; Alain C. Enthoven and K. Wayne Smith, *How Much Is Enough?: Shaping the Defense Program 1961–1969* (Santa Monica, Calif.: RAND, 2005, original publication date 1971), pp. 214–16; and John Lewis Gaddis, *Strategies of Containment* (Oxford University Press, 1982), pp. 297, 323.

7. John A. Nagl and Travis Sharp, "Operational for What?: The Future of the Guard and Reserves," *Joint Force Quarterly*, no. 59 (4th Quarter 2010), pp. 21–29; and Paul McHale, "Unreserved Support," *The American Interest* (September/October 2010), pp. 44–49.

8. See, for example, Secretary of Defense Les Aspin, *Report on the Bottom-Up Review* (Washington: Department of Defense, 1993), pp. 12–20; Thomas Donnelly, *Operation Iraqi Freedom: A Strategic Assessment* (Washington: American Enterprise Institute, 2004), pp. 32–51; Anthony H. Cordesman, *The Iraq War: Strategy, Tactics, and Military Lessons* (Washington: Center for Strategic and International Studies, 2006), pp. 37–40; Michael R. Gordon and General Bernard E. Trainor, *Cobra II: The Inside Story of the Invasion and Occupation of Iraq* (New York: Pantheon Books, 2006), pp. 38–54; and Don Oberdorfer, *The Two Koreas: A Contemporary History* (Reading, Mass.: Addison-Wesley, 1997), p. 315.

9. See Andrew F. Krepinevich, *The Quadrennial Defense Review: Rethinking the U.S. Military Posture* (Washington: Center for Strategic and Budgetary Assessments, 2005), pp. 63–65; Michael O'Hanlon, *Defense Strategy for the Post-Saddam Era* (Brookings, 2005), pp. 95–118; and Michael O'Hanlon, *Dealing with the Collapse of a Nuclear-Armed State: The Cases of North Korea and Pakistan* (Princeton, N.J.: Princeton Project on National Security, 2006).

10. Bruce E. Bechtol Jr., *Defiant Failed State: The North Korean Threat to International Security* (Dulles, Va.: Potomac Books, 2010), pp. 45–47 and 186–88.

11. See, for example, International Institute for Strategic Studies, *North Korean Security Challenges: A Net Assessment* (London, 2011), pp. 47–64.

12. Bruce W. Bennett and Jennifer Lind, "The Collapse of North Korea: Military Missions and Requirements," *International Security,* vol. 36, no. 2 (Fall 2011), pp. 107–17.

13. Kenneth M. Pollack, Daniel L. Byman, Martin Indyk, Suzanne Maloney, Michael E. O'Hanlon, and Bruce Riedel, *Which Path to Persia: Options for a New American Strategy toward Iran* (Brookings, 2009), pp. 94–98.

14. See International Institute for Strategic Studies, *The Military Balance 2012* (Oxfordshire, England, 2012), pp. 323–26; and Michael E. O'Hanlon, *The Art of War in the Age of Peace: U.S. Military Posture for the Post-Cold War World* (Westport, Conn.: Praeger, 1992), p. 68.

15. R. D. Hooker and Pedro Velica, "Iron Resolve," *RUSI Journal,* vol. 157, no. 6 (December 1, 2012), pp. 86–104; see also, on the more general subject of "punish and contain" strategies, Stuart E. Johnson, Irv Blickstein, David C. Gompert, Charles Nemfakos, Harry J. Thie, Michael J. McNerney, Duncan Long, Brian McInnis, and Amy Potter, *A Strategy-Based Framework for Accommodating Reductions in the Defense Budget* (Santa Monica, Calif.: RAND, 2012), pp. 19–20.

16. See Sumit Ganguly, *Conflict Unending: India-Pakistan Tensions Since 1947* (Columbia University Press, 2001).

17. International Institute for Strategic Studies, *The Military Balance 2011* (Oxfordshire: Routledge, 2011), p. 472; International Institute for Strategic Studies, *The Military Balance 2001–2002* (Oxford University Press, 2001), p. 299; and International Institute for Strategic Studies, *The Military Balance 1991–1992* (London: Brassey's, 1991), p. 212.

18. Thom Shanker, "Defense Secretary Warns NATO of 'Dim' Future," *New York Times,* June 10, 2011 (www.nytimes.com/2011/06/11/world/europe/11 gates.html?_r=1&emc=eta1).

19. As one example, see Choe Sang-Hun, "Island's Naval Base Stirs Opposition in South Korea," *New York Times,* August 19, 2011 (www.nytimes.com/2011/08/19/world/asia/19base.html?_r=1&emc=eta1).

20. Wendell Minnick, "CRS Report Reviews Taiwan Security, U.S. Relations," *Defense News,* May 24, 2012 (www.defensenews.com/article/2012 0524/DEFREG02/305240003/CRS-Report-Reviews-Taiwan-Security-U-S-Relations).

21. Ministry of Defence, *Defence Plan 2010–2014* (London, 2010).

Chapter 3

1. See Andrew F. Krepinevich, *Why AirSea Battle?* (Washington: Center for Strategic and Budgetary Assessments, 2010).

2. See "Statement of General James F. Amos before the House Armed Services Committee on the 2011 Posture of the United States Marine Corps," March 1, 2011, p. 13 (http://armedservices.house.gov/index.cfm/files/serve?File_id= 6e6d479e-0bea-41a1-8f3d-44b3147640fe).

3. On Russia's interests, see Marlene Laruelle, "Russian Military Presence in the High North: Projection of Power and Capacities of Action," in Stephen J. Blank, ed., *Russia in the Arctic* (Carlisle, Pa.: Strategic Studies Institute, 2011), pp. 63–89.

4. Testimony of Admiral Gary Roughead, chief of naval operations, U.S. Navy, before the House Armed Services Committee, March 1, 2011, pp. 3–5 (www.navy.mil/navydata/people/cno/Roughead/Other/110301%20HASC%20Transcript.pdf).

5. "Statement of Chief of Naval Operations Admiral Jonathan Greenert before the Congress on the FY 2013 Navy Posture," U.S. Navy, March 2012 (www.navy.mil/cno/120316_PS.pdf); and Christopher P. Cavas, "U.S. Navy Cuts Fleet Goal to 306 Ships," *Defense News*, February 4, 2013, p. 13.

6. Secretary of Defense Robert Gates, *Quadrennial Defense Review Report* (Washington: Department of Defense, February 2010), pp. 46–47.

7. See Daniel J. Franken, "Changing the Way the Navy Deploys," *Proceedings*, vol. 127, no. 1 (U.S. Naval Institute, January 2001), p. 70; Eric J. Labs, *Crew Rotation in the Navy: The Long-Term Effect on Forward Presence* (Washington: Congressional Budget Office, October 2007), p. 17; Ronald O'Rourke, "Naval Forward Deployments and the Size of the Navy" (Washington: Congressional Research Service, November 1992), pp. 13–23; and William F. Morgan, *Rotate Crews, Not Ships* (Alexandria, Va.: Center for Naval Analyses, June 1994), pp. 1–9.

8. Labs, *Crew Rotation in the Navy,* pp. 7–14.

9. Eric J. Labs, "An Analysis of the Navy's Fiscal Year 2012 Shipbuilding Plan" (Washington: Congressional Budget Office, June 2011), p. 15 (www.cbo.gov/ftpdocs/122xx/doc12237/06-23-NavyShipbuilding.pdf).

10. Lieutenant Johannes Schonberg, "Sea Swap Redux," *Proceedings,* vol. 139, no. 1 (U.S. Naval Institute, January 2013), pp. 28–33.

11. Sam Lagrone, "USN Relying on 'Cannibalisation' to Stay Afloat," *Jane's Defence Weekly,* July 27, 2011, p. 8.

12. With the fleet response program, the Navy no longer insists on scrupulously maintaining an absolutely continuous presence in the Mediterranean, Persian Gulf, and Western Pacific regions. Now it is more inclined to make

deployments unpredictable, sometimes using more and sometimes less assets than before, particularly in the Mediterranean.

13. Eric J. Labs, *Increasing the Mission Capability of the Attack Submarine Force* (Washington: Congressional Budget Office, 2002), pp. xvii, 11–13.

14. International Institute for Strategic Studies, *The Military Balance 1999–2000* (Oxford University Press, 1999), pp. 28–30; and GlobalSecurity. org, "Operation Southern Watch" (Washington, May 2011) (www. global security.org/military/ops/southern_watch.htm).

15. Congressional Budget Office, *Reducing the Deficit: Spending and Revenue Options* (Washington: Congressional Budget Office, 2011), p. 90; and Michael E. O'Hanlon, *The Science of War* (Princeton University Press, 2009), p. 26. On the potential for rivalries and conflicts within East Asia, see, for example, Robert D. Kaplan, *Monsoon* (New York: Random House, 2010); Richard C. Bush, *The Perils of Proximity* (Brookings, 2010); and Andrew S. Erickson, Walter C. Ladwig III, and Justin D. Mikolay, "Diego Garcia and the United States' Emerging Indian Ocean Strategy," *Asian Security*, vol. 6, no. 3 (September–December 2010), pp. 214–37.

16. Sam Lagrone, "USN to Go Down to Nine Carrier Strike Groups by Year's End," *Jane's Defence Weekly*, August 17, 2011, p. 9.

17. O'Hanlon, *The Science of War*, p. 78.

18. Ibid., pp. 85–103.

Chapter 4

1. P. W. Singer, "Think before You Cut," *ForeignPolicy.com*, August 11, 2011 (www.foreignpolicy.com).

2. R. William Thomas, *The Economic Effects of Reduced Defense Spending* (Washington: Congressional Budget Office, 1992), pp. 5–42.

3. Briefing by Robert H. Trice, senior vice president, Lockheed Martin, "The Business of Aerospace and Defense," Washington, D.C., September 2010, p. 8.

4. Barry D. Watts, *The U.S. Defense Industrial Base: Past, Present and Future* (Washington: Center for Strategic and Budgetary Assessments, 2008), pp. 32, 81–90.

5. Aerospace Industries Association, "The Unseen Cost: Industrial Base Consequences of Defense Strategy Choices" (Arlington, Va., July 2009), p. 1.

6. Stephen J. Hadley and William J. Perry, cochairs, "The QDR in Perspective: Meeting America's National Security Needs in the 21st Century," Quadrennial Defense Review Independent Panel (Washington, 2010), pp. 84–91 (www.usip.org/files/qdr/qdrreport.pdf).

7. Michael E. O'Hanlon, *The Science of War* (Princeton University Press, 2009), p. 30.

8. O'Hanlon, *The Science of War*, pp. 8–31; and Amy Belasco, *Paying for Military Readiness and Upkeep: Trends in Operation and Maintenance Spending* (Washington: Congressional Budget Office, 1997), pp. 5–15.

9. Hadley and Perry, "The QDR in Perspective," p. 53.

10. Statement of Christine H. Fox, director of cost assessment and program evaluation, Department of Defense, before the Senate Armed Services Committee, May 19, 2011 (www.armed-services.senate.gov/e_witnesslist.cfm?id=5213); and Andrea Shalal-Ela, "Exclusive: U.S. Sees Lifetime Cost of F-35 Fighter at $1.45 Trillion," Reuters, March 29, 2012 (www.reuters.com/article/2012/03/29/us-lockheed-fighter-idUSBRE82S03L20120329).

11. Statement of General James F. Amos before the House Armed Services Committee on the 2011 Posture of the United States Marine Corps, March 1, 2011, p. 13 (http://armedservices.house.gov/index.cfm/files/serve?File_id=6e6d479e-0bea-41a1-8f3d-44b3147640fe).

12. See Captain Henry J. Hendicks and Lt. Col. J. Noel Williams, "Twilight of the $UPERfluous Carrier," *Proceedings*, vol. 137, no. 5 (U.S. Naval Institute, May 2011) (www.usni.org/magazines/proceedings/2011-05/twilight-uperfluous-carrier).

13. Northrop Grumman,"X-47B UCAS" (Washington, 2013) (www.as.northropgrumman.com/products/nucasx47b/index.html). An additional virtue of unmanned systems is the ability to conduct training for pilots less expensively.

14. See U.S. Air Force, "Fact Sheet on MQ-9 Reaper," January 2012 (www.af.mil/information/factsheets/factsheet.asp?id=6405); and Congressional Budget Office, *Policy Options for Unmanned Aircraft Systems* (Washington: Congressional Budget Office, June 2011), pp. ix–x (www.cbo.gov/sites/default/files/cbofiles/ftpdocs/121xx/doc12163/06-08-uas.pdf).

15. These are ongoing; see Bill Carey, "F-35 Delay Forces $3 Billion Upgrade Request for U.S. Air Force F-16s," AINOnline, November 4, 2011 (www.ainonline.com/aviation-news/ain-defense-perspective/2011-11-04/f-35-delay-forces-3-billion-upgrade-request-us-air-force-f-16s).

16. Leithen Francis, "Mission Impossible," *Aviation Week and Space Technology*, August 15, 2011, p. 27.

17. The chief of naval operations, while not abandoning support for the F-35C, has nonetheless voiced some doubts about the central role of stealth in future force planning. See Admiral Jonathan W. Greenert, "Payloads over Platforms: Charting a New Course," *Proceedings*, vol. 138, no. 7 (U.S. Naval Institute, July 2012) (www.usni.org/magazines/proceedings/2012-07/payloads-over-platforms-charting-new-course).

18. See P. W. Singer, *Wired for War: The Robotics Revolution and Conflict in the 21st Century* (New York: Penguin Press, 2009); and Michael E. O'Hanlon, *Technological Change and the Future of Warfare* (Brookings, 2000), p. 65.

19. For a good historical example of such a case, see Montgomery C. Meigs, *Slide Rules and Submarines: American Scientists and Subsurface Warfare in*

World War II (University Press of the Pacific, 2002); on the more general challenge of promoting innovation within military bureaucracies, see, for example, Stephen Peter Rosen, *Winning the Next War* (Cornell University Press, 1991).

20. The Nunn-McCurdy Amendment to the 1982 Defense Authorization Act triggers reviews of weapons when their estimated program cost exceeds original estimates by 50 percent. See Department of Defense, "Selected Acquisition Report (SAR) Summary Tables" (Washington, April 2, 2010), p. 3 (www.acq.osd.mil/ara/2009%20DEC%20SAR.pdf).

21. On cost savings estimates, see Congressional Budget Office, *Budget Options* (Washington: Congressional Budget Office, 2009), pp. 5–21 (www.cbo.gov/ftpdocs/102xx/doc10294/08-06-BudgetOptions.pdf); Department of Defense, "Selected Acquisition Report (SAR) Summary Tables" (Washington: Congressional Budget Office, December 31, 2009), pp. 21–23 (www.acq.osd.mil/ara/2009%20DEC%20SAR.pdf); and Michael E. O'Hanlon, *A Skeptic's Case for Nuclear Disarmament* (Brookings, 2010), pp. 110–31.

22. See "Pentagon Admits: Navy's Newest Warship Can't Survive Combat," RT, January 17, 2013 (http://rt.com/usa/news/combat-ship-navy-freedom-163/).

23. Commander John Patch, "The Wrong Ship at the Wrong Time," *Proceedings,* vol. 137, no. 1 (U.S. Naval Institute, January 2011), pp. 16–19 (www.usni.org/ magazines/proceedings/2011-01/wrong-ship-wrong-time); and Lexington Institute, "Countering the Asymmetric Threat from Sea Mines" (Alexandria, Va., March 2010).

Chapter 5

1. Steven Pifer and Michael O'Hanlon, *The Opportunity: Next Steps in Reducing Nuclear Arms* (Brookings, 2012).

2. Tom Z. Collina, "U.S. Nuclear Modernization Programs," Arms Control Association (Washington, August 2012) (www.armscontrol.org/factsheets/USNuclearModernization).

3. Arnie Heller, "Plutonium at 150 Years: Going Strong and Aging Gracefully," *Science and Technology Review* (December 2012), pp. 11–15. Los Alamos's pit production capacities could be modernized and upgraded modestly at a total cost of less than $1 billion; see Tom Z. Collina, "Longer Life Seen for Warhead Pits," *Arms Control Today,* vol. 43, no. 1 (January/February 2013), pp. 42–43.

4. Tom Z. Collina, "Rising Costs for B61 Prompt Questions," *Arms Control Today,* vol. 42, no. 10 (December 2012), pp. 31–32.

5. For the cost estimates, see Michael O'Hanlon, *A Skeptic's Case for Nuclear Disarmament* (Brookings, 2010).

6. Congressional Budget Office, *Reducing the Deficit: Spending and Revenue Options* (Washington, Congressional Budget Office, March 2011), p. 96 (www.cbo.gov/sites/default/files/cbofiles/ftpdocs/120xx/doc12085/03-10-reducingthedeficit.pdf).

7. Roger Z. George, "Reflections on CIA Analysis: Is It Finished?" *Intelligence and National Security,* vol. 26, no. 1 (February 2011), pp. 72–81.

8. Ken Dilanian, "Overall U.S. Intelligence Budget Tops $80 Billion," *Los Angeles Times,* October 28, 2010 (http://articles.latimes.com/2010/oct/28/nation/la-na-intel-budget-20101029).

9. Richard K. Betts, *Enemies of Intelligence: Knowledge and Power in American National Security* (Columbia University Press, 2007).

10. Deputy Secretary of Defense William J. Lynn III, "A Military Strategy for the New Space Environment," *Washington Quarterly,* vol. 34, no. 3 (Summer 2011), pp. 10–12.

11. See Dana Priest and William M. Arkin, "A Hidden World, Growing beyond Control," *Washington Post,* July 19, 2010 (http://projects.washingtonpost.com/top-secret-america/articles/a-hidden-world-growing-beyond-control/print).

Chapter 6

1. Robert F. Hale, speech at the Brookings Institution, January 7, 2013 (www.brookings.edu/~/media/events/2013/1/07%20defense%20spending/20130117_defense_sequestration.pdf).

2. Congressional Budget Office, "Costs of Military Pay and Benefits in the Defense Budget" (Washington: Congressional Budget Office, November 2012), p. 21. (www.cbo.gov/sites/default/files/cbofiles/attachments/11-14-12-Military Comp_0.pdf).

3. Bruce Newsome, *Made, Not Born: Why Some Soldiers Are Better than Others* (Westport, Conn.: Praeger, 2007). Some changes are already being made to reduce training modestly; see "Operational Training Rates," *Air Force Magazine* (April 2011), p. 69.

4. Department of Defense, *Report of the Eleventh Quadrennial Review of Military Compensation* (2012), pp. 26–29 (Militarypay.defense.gov/REPORTS/QRMC/11th_QRMC_Main_Report_Linked.pdf).

5. Congressional Budget Office, "Costs of Military Pay and Benefits in the Defense Budget," p. 2.

6. On cost savings estimates, see Congressional Budget Office, *Budget Options* (Washington: Congressional Budget Office, 2009), pp. 24–25 (www.cbo.gov/ftpdocs/102xx/doc10294/08-06-BudgetOptions.pdf).

7. Ibid., pp. 28–29.

8. See Secretary of Defense Robert M. Gates, remarks at American Enterprise Institute, May 24, 2011 (www.aei.org /files/2011/05/24/SECDEF-AEI-Remarks.pdf); Congressional Budget Office, *The Effects of Proposals to Increase Cost-Sharing in TRICARE* (Washington, Congressional Budget Office, 2009), p. 4; and Karl Gingrich, "Making It Personnel: The Need for Military Compensation Reform," Brookings Institution, February 2012 (www.brookings.edu/~/media/research/files/papers/2012/2/military%20compensation%20gingrich/02_military_compensation_gingrich.pdf).

9. Stephen J. Hadley and William J. Perry, cochairs, "The QDR in Perspective: Meeting America's National Security Needs in the 21st Century," Quadrennial Defense Review Independent Panel (Washington, 2010) (www.usip.org/files/qdr/qdrreport.pdf).

10. Defense Business Board, "Modernizing the Military Retirement System," July 21, 2011, p. 18 (www.slideshare.net/BrianLucke/modernizing-the-military-retirement-system).

11. Marcus Weisgerber and Kate Brannen, "Gates Details $13.6 Billion in DoD Cuts," *Defense News*, March 21, 2011, p. 1 (www.defensenews.com/apps/pbcs.dll/article?AID=2011103210310).

12. Government Accountability Office, "Military Base Realignments and Closures: Updated Costs and Savings Estimates from BRAC 2005," GAO-12-709R (Washington: Government Accountability Office, June 29, 2012), pp. 1–5 (www.gao.gov/assets/600/592076.pdf).

13. Robert F. Hale, speech at the Brookings Institution.

14. For historical perspective, see, for example, G. Wayne Glass, "Closing Military Bases: An Interim Assessment" (Washington: Congressional Budget Office, December 1996), p. 63.

15. Charles S. Clark, "Pentagon Acquisition Chief Focuses on Workforce amid Budget Challenges," *Government Executive*, November 14, 2012 (www.govexec.com/contracting/2012/11/pentagon-acquisition-chief-focuses-workforce-amid-budget-challenges/59509/).

16. Government Accountability Office, "Strategic Sourcing: Improved and Expanded Use Could Save Billions in Annual Procurement Costs," GAO-12-919 (Washington: Government Accountability Office, September 2012), pp. 11–13 (www.gao.gov/assets/650/648644.pdf).

17. See comments by Jack Mayer at panel discussion with Col. John Barnett, Jack Mayer, Bill Moore, and Nick Avdellas, Brookings Institution, January 22, 2013 (www.brookings.edu/events/2013/01/24-defense-spending#ref-id=20130124_ohanlon).

18. Government Accountability Office, "Defense Acquisitions: Further Action Needed to Improve DoD's Insight and Management of Long-Term Main-

tenance Contracts," GAO-12-558 (Washington: Government Accountability Office, May 2012), pp. 1–8 (www.gao.gov/assets/600/591319.pdf).

19. See panel discussion with Col. John Barnett, Jack Mayer, Bill Moore, and Nick Avdellas, Brookings Institution, January 24, 2013 (www.brookings.edu/~/media/events/2013/1/24%20defense%20spending/20130124_defense_spending_transcript.pdf).

20. For a similar type of list, see Hadley and Perry, "The QDR in Perspective," pp. 67–79.

21. For related views from the Defense Business Board, see John T. Burnett, "Panel: DoD Should Cut 111,000 Civilian Jobs," *Federal Times,* July 26, 2010, p. 1.

22. For one discussion of this, see Michele A. Flournoy, "The Right Way to Cut Pentagon Spending," *Wall Street Journal,* February 5, 2013, p. 15.

23. For one good argument for keeping forces in Europe, see John R. Deni, *The Future of American Landpower: Does Forward Presence Still Matter? The Case of the Army in Europe* (Carlisle, Pa.: Strategic Studies Institute, 2012).

24. Government Accountability Office, "Defense Management: Comprehensive Cost Information and Analysis of Alternatives Needed to Assess Military Posture in Asia" (Washington: Government Accountability Office, May 2011) (www.gao.gov/new.items/d11316.pdf).

25. Walter Pincus, "Senator Tom Coburn Cuts the Fat at the Pentagon in His 'Department of Everything' Report," *Washington Post,* November 19, 2012.

INDEX